PSYCHOLOGY FROM THE HEART

PSYCHOLOGY FROM THE HEART

The Spiritual Depth of Clinical Psychology

Raymond Lloyd Richmond, Ph.D.

ISBN-13: 978-1467907651
ISBN-10: 1467907650

CONTENTS

INTRODUCTION

IN his masterful play, *Man and Superman*, George Bernard Shaw turned the classical images of heaven and hell upside down. He described hell as a place of complete satisfaction, where all desires are freely fulfilled. Personal responsibility had no place in hell. It did in heaven, though, a place for the "masters of reality"—and, curiously enough, the place where souls were free to go when they finally got sick of hell.

This is a provocative metaphor. Being a metaphor, though, it is not to be taken literally in a metaphysical sense. But it is a good metaphor for how we live our life in *this* world, because this concept of "a hell that you can leave when you get sick of it" aptly describes psychological change as well. Many people cling to their own psychological "hell," no matter how painful it may be, because the discipline of health is even more fearful. But eventually, if they catch only a glimpse of sorrow for the mess they're in, they can get sick of it all and decide to cross over to "reality."

Therefore, though an atheist, not a theologian, Shaw nevertheless made a brilliant discovery: *a spiritual life is also a practical life.* Yet such practicality does not depend on *knowledge* so much as *understanding.*

Too many persons today, however, preoccupy themselves with knowledge, whether it be intellectual or carnal, and in doing so they sidestep the concept of understanding. Why? Because understanding involves "standing under something," and that something is the "law"—not the local penal code, but the psychological law of lack and limitation that holds the agony of *being* itself as it stands on the brink of redemption through divine love. All the pages of knowledge flap uselessly in the swirling gusts that blow along that ridge.

This lack and limitation affects every child born into this world, because we are all born into a pre-existing social world of language, science, technology, art, literature, and so on that excludes us and mystifies us. But even more profound than the mystery of the sum total of all this factual information is the mystery of the child's own body. The child finds itself literally at the mercy of biological processes—eating, vomiting, defecation, urination, bleeding, reproduction, and death—that it can neither control nor comprehend. Thus the child will feel excluded and will believe—rightly so—that the world "knows" something that he or she does not know. Right from the beginning, then, the child is located in a profound emotional space of "not knowing" and feeling "left out."

Moreover, when children are criticized and humiliated by

others, they can develop the belief that others are *deliberately* withholding knowledge from them, and this belief can cause the children to burn with anger at their parents in particular and at the world in general. Such children can develop an intense desperation to want to figure out everything in advance, before risking doing anything, so as to avoid further feelings of humiliation.

Knowing—that is, anticipating—what might happen next is a characteristic defensive desire of children in dysfunctional families. After all, if they can guess an irrational parent's next move, they might be able to avoid an ugly family scene.

To such children, then, it's a loathsome thing to admit, "I don't know."

This explains why, if you offer some piece of information to a person who grew up in a dysfunctional family, his or her response will not be a simple "Thank you" but will be a quickly retorted "I know!"

It's an awkward, uncomfortable, and frustrating place to be—and so we all devote considerable energy to overcoming the feeling of "not knowing."

- We might seek out intellectual knowledge through formal education.

- We might engage in scientific research.

- We might join country clubs, gangs, cults, cliques, or any other social organization that purports to offer some secret "knowledge."

- We might search through myriads of pornographic images hoping for the special privilege of seeing what is usually kept hidden.

- We might seek out "carnal knowledge" through the body of another person and attempt to locate the psychological agony of our bodily mystery in the pleasure—or pain—of the "other."

- We might create our own fantasy worlds—with thoughts and images of eroticism, heroism, revenge, or destruction—in which we can "figure it out" on our own so as to possess the power and recognition we so desperately crave.

However much we might desire it, all the "knowledge" in the world is nothing but a thin veil that hangs over the dark anguish of helplessly "not knowing." Standing before the veil, suspecting the secret truth of our "not knowing," we feel confused, disgusted, weak, useless, and deceived.

 The brilliant French psychoanalyst, Jacques Lacan, in *The Four Fundamental Concepts of Psycho-Analysis*, tells the story of a competition between two ancient painters, Zeuxis and Parrhasios.[1] Zeuxis receives acclaim for painting grapes so life-like that even the birds who try to peck at them are fooled. In his pride, Zeuxis then goes to look at the work of Parrhasios. But Zeuxis sees only a veil, and so he asks to see the painting that Parrhasios has hidden behind the veil. Well, Parrhasios' painting *was* the veil. It was so well done that it fooled even the master of deceptive painting himself. Hence Lacan points out that if you want to deceive someone, present him with a "veil," something that incites his pride to want to know what is being hidden from him.

With all of our knowledge hanging like a deceptive veil over the agony of being, then, we stand helplessly under the psychological law of lack and limitation. Trapped in this wretched state, therefore, we have only one hope: to understand the soul.

Psychologically speaking, to paraphrase Lacan, *soul* is something—alien to the mundane—that empowers us to bear what is intolerable and lacking in the human world.[2]

In this modern world, though, much of our society has lost its sense of soul. In the collective desire for diversity it's all too easy to misunderstand life by confusing the truth of *tolerance* with the fraud of *acceptance*, the truth of *holiness* with the fraud of *pride*, and the truth of *love* with the fraud of *sensuality*.

Furthermore, with the loss of soul many of us today have

also discarded the concept of *sin*—which, in psychological language, is the functional narcissism in all of us which serves the self, rather than others. So, instead of making life's decisions according to personal responsibility, we make decisions according to personal convenience. Sin, therefore, is what blinds us to the realization that there's more to life than the veil of the psychological "self" that the world shows us as the coveted image of *happiness*. As such, sin pulls us away from real love and sucks us down into the hedonistic mire of narcissism—and there, in that foul netherworld, soul is lost.

Sin may be convenient, but it's just not practical.

The great theologian Augustine of Hippo, in north Africa, said that "Sin is the punishment of sin." This makes perfect sense if you understand that the human social world is nothing but a mass of psychological defenses—pride, anger, competition, social status, take your pick—which protect us in our blindness, the blindness that results from an ignorance of soul. All defenses originate in childhood as ways to assist survival, but carried on unconsciously into adulthood those same defenses—the ones that once protected us—lead us into nothing but the repeated punishment of psychological and social dysfunction.

Don't misunderstand this. We are all basically good. But goodness takes work—lots of work. Hard work. And self-restraint. For without our restraining the pride of self and its defenses, real love, the most exquisite and pure love imaginable, remains invisible. Along the path of least re-sistance—the path of sin, the easy way, the way to no-where—love is nowhere to be seen, for it remains ban-ished behind the thorny hedges of psychological defenses. And what is real love, if not to give of yourself to save oth-ers—even those who hate you— from their blindness?

We would do well, then, to pay attention to sin today while remembering that crossing the barrier between sin and spirituality is a simple matter of personal choice, with complete freedom to go in either direction. Psychology has too often been preoccupied with the pursuit of happi-ness, and it has missed the point about helping individu-als understand life and find a personally meaningful—and practical—sense of direction. Psychology itself cannot of-fer any meaning to life, but it can help individuals disen-tangle themselves from the snare of illusory social identi-fications that keep us trapped in spiritual blindness and pull us backwards into self-destruction.

I can offer no "proof" of God, nor can I prove that souls exist or that spirituality is anything more than a figment of our imaginations. But look at it this way: If you value spirituality, what do you have to lose? Mediocrity. What do you have to gain? Everything.

NOTES

1. Jacques Lacan, "The Four Fundamental Concepts of

Psycho-Analysis." Edited by Jacques-Alain Miller, translated by Alan Sheridan. (New York: W. W. Norton, 1981). See p. 103 and pp. 111-112.

2. Jacques Lacan, "A Love Letter." In Mitchell, J. & Rose, J. (Eds.), *Feminine Sexuality: Jacques Lacan and the école freudienne*. (New York: W. W. Norton [paperback], 1985). See p. 155:

> "And yet I fail to see why the fact of having a soul should be a scandal for thought—were it true. If it were true, the soul could only be spoken as whatever enables a being . . . to bear what is intolerable in its world, which presumes this soul to be alien to that world. . . ."

1 ANGER

THE TRUTH is, anger may be a "natural"—that is, a commonly occurring—social reaction to hurt and insult, but being natural doesn't make it good for us. Sure, "natural" foods are commonly advertised as being healthy and good for us. But poisons, for example, are also natural, and poisons, by definition, are deadly.

There are far better ways to cope with hurt and insult than with anger, because anger itself acts like a poison in your own heart that ultimately degrades the quality of your own life as much as it hurts the life of another person.

WE all feel hurt or irritated when someone or something obstructs our needs or desires. Anger, though, is not truly an emotion. In its technical sense, anger refers to the desire to "get even with"—that is, to take revenge on—the cause of the hurt.

ALL anger is, at its core, a dark and cruel wish for harm to come upon the person who hurt you.

WHEN you carry your feelings of irritation a step beyond mere feelings and into the realm of *desire for revenge*, you enter into evil; that is, anger becomes evil when you actually inflict hurt on someone in return for the hurt inflicted on you. This revenge is an expression of *hatred* because it seeks the other's harm rather than the other's good.

A COMMON way to block out unpleasant and frightening emotions, especially emotions of helplessness, is with anger, allowing free reign to impulses of hatred and revenge. When you get angry you don't really allow yourself to feel your inner vulnerability and hurt. All you can think about in the moment is your desire to get revenge, to defend your pride, to do something—anything—to create the feeling that you have power and importance. In essence, your outbursts of rage paradoxically hide your inner feelings of vulnerability, so you never *recognize* the *hurt* you're feeling that triggers your hostile reaction. All the bitterness and hostility is a big puff of smoke, an emotional fraud. It hardens your heart toward others so that you can seal off your own emotional pain.

YOU have good reason to be angry, but, as I said before, you are blind to your anger. You have done such a good job of hiding it from others that you have hidden it from yourself to such an extent that you deny it even exists.

REVENGE can be enacted both actively and passively. It can be enacted actively through hostility, cursing, sarcasm, sexuality (adultery, promiscuity, pornography, etc.), or disobedience. It can also be enacted passively through disobedience as well as through self-sabotage, drug or alcohol abuse, obesity, smoking, suicidal impulses, masturbation, or the inability to achieve goals.

But, just as with hiding the hurt, revenge does not heal the hurt either. That's because all hurt, at its core, is simply a reminder of your essential human vulnerability and helplessness. Even if you kill the person who hurts you, you still remain vulnerable to another attack from someone else. With all revenge, then, you might temporarily feel powerful, but the feeling is just an illusion. No matter what you do, you remain vulnerable to attack from anyone, anywhere.

So, not knowing how to manage anger in a spiritually healthy manner, you stifled your awareness of your anger by stifling your emotional life. You didn't eliminate emotions entirely (because no one can), yet you stifled your feelings sufficiently to convince yourself that what you were feeling was somehow wrong, or in error, or unnecessary, or of no real purpose. You learned to function in the intellectual realm, seeking out reasons and explanations—learning every polemic in the book—to allow you to ward off your emotional hurt. You did what many children do. You hardened your heart sufficiently to the emotional pain of yourself and others to protect yourself from your anger while still allowing you a sense of duty to carry out your responsibilities.

You did this all, not realizing that, in denying your own feelings, you were essentially cheating yourself of the very love your father denied you.

You might feel hurt by someone emotionally close to you, and, out of fear that your immediate impulse to hurt that person in return will cause you to lose that person's "love," you suppress the awareness of your honest inner experiences. If you do this often enough you can end up convincing yourself that everything is fine and peaceful. In this case the hurt becomes anger *anyway*, only it becomes *unconscious anger*: you remain hurt while the desire to hurt the other person gets pushed into your unconscious where it stews in bitter resentment. And so, in reality, you are just deceiving yourself and defiling your relationships when you deny that you have anything to feel hurt about. And before you know it you're wondering why you're so depressed. Depression, after all, is often "anger turned inwards"—that is, you end up despising yourself because you feel guilty for unconsciously wanting to hurt someone else.

You need to realize that any damage that was ever done to you has in turn led you to damage others. Those who are hated learn to hate; those who are abused learn, if not to abuse, at least to hold on to anger, a lack of trust, and an unconscious desire for revenge.

Because anger is not a feeling, it is possible to "be" angry even though you do not feel anything. This is the problem with unconscious anger: you don't feel the anger, so, even as it works its poison in you and toward others, you believe it isn't even there.

NOW, why would you be angry with your parents? Well, you're angry with them because of their failures in leading you into a proper knowing of the world. You're angry because you were left having to figure out everything for yourself. As a child, you wanted nurturing, guidance, explanations, and emotional and physical protection, but for one reason or another your parents failed you. They may have been absent physically or emotionally, and in that absence they essentially disabled you psychologically and spiritually.

SOME persons cling with unconscious determination to a childlike desire to make their parents admit their mistakes. These persons use their own disability as evidence of their parents' failures—evidence to be thrown back into their parents' faces—and, in so doing, they effectively reject divine love for the savor of revenge.

"What?" you ask. "Revenge? That's ridiculous. I don't want revenge. I'm past that."

Well, no one is "past" the capacity for self-deception, and only when you can be honest about your entanglement in the unconscious can you extricate yourself from it. So, if you truly were past revenge, you would do *anything* it takes—pay any price and overcome any fear—to be healed, and then you would turn to your parents and, as a gift of real love, offer to them your healing, as evidence that, despite all their mistakes, they really didn't cripple you forever. But by continuing in your self-sabotaging behavior you show that you would prefer to send yourself to hell just to prove to others how much they have hurt you. It's simply impossible to open yourself to God's healing grace until you let go of the secret hope that your own self-destruction will bring you the sweet satisfaction of . . . well, revenge.

BECAUSE of the way your parents treated you, you fear love—and, because you fear love, you have been suppressing your anger just enough to keep it out of sight but not enough to prevent it from leaking out when you are most vulnerable. In your case, you are most vulnerable when others' lack of respect for your sense of duty causes you to catch a momentary glimpse of the truth that *duty is not love*. Your anger is just a puff of smoke—a magician's trick—that allows you to quickly remove from sight your lack of love for God and replace it with your indignation that others lack love for God.

AFTER scrutinizing their childhood, some persons will say that they feel sad or lonely but do not feel any anger at their parents. In these cases, the anger can be recognized not through the emotion of rage but through specific *behaviors of hate*.

Hatred for authority can be expressed through criminal activity; political protest and terrorism; pornography; abortion; shoplifting; speeding; being late for appointments; living in clutter or filth; etc.

Hatred for the self can be expressed through the self-sabotage of one's potential such as by chronic procrastination; the inability to support oneself by working; over-dependence on others; substance abuse; obesity; codependence (such as marrying an alcoholic); emotional disability; etc.

But whether the end result be hatred for authority or hatred for yourself, the underlying cause of your behavior is anger at your parents, because of their failures in love.

IN the unconscious, the anger gets distorted because it is difficult for children to be angry with a father from whom they still desire a sign of love. To protect themselves from this dilemma, their unconscious finds an ingenious solution to raw, dangerous anger: *do nothing.*

- Addictions (such as alcoholism, drug addiction, obesity, smoking, marijuana use, video games, casinos, etc.) allow them to feel filled when they are really empty; thus they *feel nothing.*

- Argumentativeness prevents them from accepting truth, which includes the truth that their father has failed them; thus they *accept nothing.*

- Being late for appointments and meetings prevents them from having to wait; thus they *wait for nothing.*

- Immodesty (whether as revealing clothing,

gaudy make-up, tattoos, piercings, etc.) prevents them from respecting their own bodies; thus they *respect nothing*.

- Learning disorders prevent them from discovering a world that seems hidden from them; thus they *discover nothing*.

- Mental confusion (often expressed by forgetting things or as difficulty with math) prevents them from engaging with the signs and symbols of life; thus they *engage with nothing*.

- Procrastination prevents them from stepping out into the world they don't know how to negotiate in the first place; thus they *accomplish nothing*.

- Sexual preoccupation (whether as self-created mental fantasies, pornography, lust, or sexual acts) prevents them from experiencing emotional intimacy; thus they are *intimate with nothing*.

- Suspiciousness prevents them from having to trust a world they fear; thus they *trust nothing*.

In the end, all these "nothings," taken together, lead to the nothingness of death: on the one hand, *symbolic death*, which keeps a child emotionally disabled as punishment for his or her anger, and, on the other hand, *real death*—through slow self-sabotage or through outright suicide—by which the child, in making herself or himself the "missing one," draws attention away from the truth that the father has been missing from the child's life all along.

There is no current psychiatric diagnosis for this collection of symptoms, so I have named a psychoanalytic diagnosis: *Ira Patrem Latebrosa* (hidden anger at the father). This is an anger at the father that so cloaks itself in invisibility that a person afflicted with it will deny that it even exists.

Yet it does exist, and the evidence above proves it, like tracks in the snow that reveal the presence of an animal lurking nearby.

THE eating disorder of *Anorexia Nervosa*, which has afflicted you, is an expression of unconscious hatred for your father. You know that arbitrary authority is all a fraud. You therefore are angry with your father—and, by extension, you are angry with all authority, even legitimate authority, including even God—and you express that anger by trying to control your own body.

"BUT wait," you say, "I have no issues with my father. We got along well together. My mother was the cruel one." In that case, don't be deceived by sentimentality. Yes, you have to resolve a lot of anger at your mother—and, in addition to that, you will find considerable unconscious anger at your father: for being too physically ill, too mentally ill, or just too weak or cowardly to stop your mother's abuse.

OUR culture teaches us by example—despite its common sentimental claims about the value of peace—that insult merits immediate revenge. Thus, many persons blindly follow the path of violence—and in so doing, they "get angry" to avoid feeling the hurt that holds the acknowledgment of their own vulnerability.

SO, is there ever such a thing as "justifiable" anger? No. There is such a thing as justifiable irritation, because all irritation is an honest emotional reaction to some insult or obstruction. When your irritation progresses into anger, however, your desire to harm another person reduces you to the same level of rudeness as the person who offended you. Thus you may as well attack yourself for being rude. And, ultimately, that is exactly what you do, because the anger in your mind becomes poison in your heart that harms you as much as it harms anyone else.

CONSIDER what motivates a bully. In his own home, a child is physically abused, emotionally tormented, or both. He feels helpless and insecure. So he seeks out other children less powerful than him to bully; in doing so, he compensates for his fundamental insecurity by generating a feeling of confidence through his wielding power over others. Psychologically, it doesn't matter to him that an unfair advantage over others weaker than himself makes his power unscrupulous; all that matters to him is his feeling of satisfaction in triumph.

But is the bully really angry with the innocent children he torments? Well, no, clearly, because he literally has to go looking for trouble; that is, he's not responding to any hurt that other children cause him. So where is source of the bully's real anger? It goes back to his home—usually to his father in particular—where he has been tormented. Thus the bully takes out his anger at his father indirectly; he can't attack his father directly because his father is too psychologically dangerous, so he attacks others who are psychologically safer targets.

YES, we can even direct our anger at things. If a tool breaks right in the middle of an important task, leaving us feeling frustrated and helpless, we will smash the tool onto the floor and curse it. We "know" that damaging the tool won't fix anything, so why do we act with such aggression? Well, in "hurting" the tool—whether symbolically (that is, with curses) or physically—we receive the *satisfaction* of feeling more powerful than something else. It's as if we are thinking, in our unconscious logic, "My plans have been frustrated, and my pride has been injured, but if I can damage something—anything—then look here and see how powerful I am!"

IT'S ironic, then, that a healthy response to feelings of hurt and insult actually leads to compassion and peace, while the suppression of emotions, in trying to protect the surface peace, only leads to a psychological undercurrent of suspicion and cruelty. That's why people who become social "doormats" and let others walk all over them, rather than admit that they feel hurt about anything, usually have quite a lot of resentment and "dirt" underneath their appearance of welcome.

WHEN you are told to acknowledge your anger in psychotherapy, however, you are not being told to do something that is morally wrong. Nor are you being encouraged to "get angry," such as by yelling, cursing, throwing things, breaking things, or hitting someone. Instead, you are being told to recognize something that is *already within you*, so that you can stop deceiving yourself about your own reality.

BUT it's not easy. Hatred and revenge are such sweet delicacies in our culture that hardly anyone wants to let go of them. Yet giving up revenge and committing yourself to a life of pure love is your only choice—other than sending yourself to hell to get your revenge.

THOSE who know real love act with confidence, straightforwardness, and honesty, whereas those who present themselves as nice are often merely hiding the depths of their anger behind a show of smiling appeasement.

2 COMPETITION

THEOLOGICAL writers have been saying for ages that each person must fight the spiritual battle in his own heart, without regard for what others do. If you're always comparing yourself to others—whether at work or in recreation—you will either be feeling inferior and jealous or superior and proud. Only when you stop concerning yourself with what others are doing can you be truly humble.

WHEN the Greeks built a gymnasium in Jerusalem during the Maccabean Dynasty, the Jews were scandalized, and it holds even more true today that sports are a scandal to spirituality because you simply cannot present love to the world through the evil-for-evil and insult-for-insult nature of strife and competition.

IMAGINE playing ping-pong without hitting the ball back, so that the other person can accumulate all the points he wants. Imagine playing bridge without doing anything to obstruct the other players in claiming all the points they want. Imagine two teams of men joyfully walking from one end of a field to the other, helping each other to accumulate all the goals they want. In the eyes of the world, it would be boring, wouldn't it? Well, in the eyes of the world, real love is boring.

So what does a person learn from childhood experiences other than that this is a world of competition, strife, and conflict, geared toward the survival of the "fittest"—or in today's world, the meanest—in which honesty and compassion are foolish weakness?

Once you strip the concept of "relationship" of its holy dignity and reduce it essentially to a self-satisfying sport—a game designed to drown out your emotional loneliness—then you place yourself on the playing field as a blatant sexual object in full competition with all the other players. Any woman who has a more pretty face or larger breasts or more shapely legs, or who is taller or thinner or more rich or more socially connected or more glamorous or more fashionably dressed is, by definition, a rival and a threat to your security. And even if in anger you try to assault the gaze of the world with body fat, tattoos, body piercings galore, and purple hair, you don't really leave the playing field, you just take up new, sometimes covert, tactics in the competitive game.

It cannot be said more simply or more clearly: Competition is fundamentally opposed to love.

3   CULTURE

IN this modern world, much of our society has lost its sense of soul. In the collective desire for diversity it's all too easy to misunderstand life by confusing the truth of *tolerance* with the fraud of *acceptance*, the truth of *holiness* with the fraud of *pride*, and the truth of *love* with the fraud of *sensuality*.

TODAY we live in a world that has so forsaken the divine that most individuals now extol *trivialities* so as to provide an illusion that their lives have *some* meaning.

THE modern quest for cultural diversity has been distorted into such a neurotic obsession with being "open" and "accepting" that we are terrified of being labeled "judgmental." If you dare to speak the truth about sin, you may be called "haughty" and "arrogant" and lacking in compassion—and you may even be told that you have a mental disorder!

IN a permissive, self-indulgent society, there is less and less use for self-discipline and self-restraint. When anything goes, nothing means anything, and all paths lead nowhere. And right in the middle of nowhere you are sure to find anxiety, depression, and distress.

So there you are, like a sheep without a shepherd, free to pursue your own self-interests—and vulnerable to the self-interest of any wolf that happens along.

Do not be deceived. There is nothing in popular culture today that encourages us to holiness, and there is everything in popular culture today that incites us to turn from God to idolize the "self" and its fleeting satisfactions.

The real problem with violent movies and music is not to be found in the matter of simple imitation; the real problem is that violent entertainment has subversive psychological effects that lead to social disintegration.

First, such forms of entertainment are popular because they allow teenagers to experience an outward expression of the very same anger and frustration they are already feeling inwardly because of their dysfunctional family lives. Keep in mind here that the expression of hostile feelings and impulses has no healing quality; instead, it only "fans the flames" of inner confusion and discontent.

Second, such forms of entertainment have a tendency to "infect" us with their destructive values of hostility, revenge, and vulgarity.

Have you ever read news reports about big snow storms and how churches cancel services because travel is too dangerous? Yet people will still flock to football games and shopping malls in that same, dangerous weather. Now, when people would forsake prayer to go to a sporting event, it's not very difficult to determine what they believe to be most real and precious in their lives, is it?

THE fact is, in many of our attempts to enjoy ourselves we end up stepping all over other persons. In seeking wealth we envy and compete with our neighbors, we exploit and deceive the underprivileged, and we pollute our God-given environment. In seeking entertainment we encourage an industry that seduces our entire culture with frivolity, vanity, and pride. In seeking sexual pleasure we spread emotional wounds, physical disease, lust, infidelity, divorce, pornography, and prostitution, along with unwanted pregnancies, abortion, foster care horrors, and child abuse. In seeking excitement we create addictions and brew a criminal underground to distribute the materials of addiction. In seeking happiness we're like the eye of a hurricane, seemingly calm and peaceful, yet blind to the storm spreading chaos all around us.

YET most individuals, because of the emotional wounds of their childhood, have more anger within their unconscious than there is oil under the rocks of the earth. And just like oil in the rocks, unconscious anger has so insidiously infiltrated our culture that every aspect of our daily life is soaked in anger, where it seeps out in cynicism, sarcasm, argumentativeness, arrogance, competition, meanness, hostility, and you-name-it. It all comes from the deep pain of emotional wounds, it all leaks out as hatred, and it poisons the heart with the sin of spiritual murder.

JACQUES Lacan, a brilliant French psychoanalyst, taught that, in psychological terms, the social world is a fraud. In so far as the social world around us places constant demands upon us as individuals, Lacan called the social world "the Other," and he expressed the truth of social fraud with a profound saying: "There is no Other of the Other." By this he meant that all of the meaning we attribute to our human creations, including language itself, has no value beyond its own reference.

Interestingly enough, the book of Genesis (2:19–20) essentially says the same thing when it tells the story about God bringing the "various wild animals and various birds of the air" to the man "to see what he would call them." Note that God didn't name the animals; He simply said that "whatever the man called each of them would be its name." Here God gave the man the freedom to create language, a language guaranteed only by its own enunciation.

Now, although Genesis speaks from the revealed religion of the Jewish tradition, and though Lacan was not religious and spoke from the position of secular psychology, the essential point should be clear: no language—indeed, no human creation—has any absolute meaning.

THE world offers itself to us in full spectacle, but there is nothing to see except a deluded man who calls himself "Emperor" standing naked in the street. Thus we have a world filled with

- Advertisers and politicians who don't fulfill their promises;

- Authority figures who have risen to their own personal level of incompetence;

- Educational systems that fail to educate;

- An entertainment industry that brainwashes us and our children into the deepest levels of perversion, all in the guise of making us "feel good";

- Health care systems that know only illness and neither understand nor care about health;

- Justice systems that are unjust;

- Parents who not only don't know how to parent but also don't even care to learn;

- Political activists who use intolerance and protest to demand tolerance and peace;

- And, yes, all of us who refuse to defend the truth but instead stay within the box of social fraud, playing its games to protect our own pride and to seek our own social status.

NOW, in the pure sense of the word, a "game" refers to a process of social interaction that depends on procedural rules to ensure that all participants know what to expect of each other. If you were playing chess and your opponent suddenly pulled out a gun and shot you, you would be at a clear disadvantage.

Therefore, because any participant interested only in the acquisition of power will dominate the others, games require rules of conduct to provide a certain fairness, so that true expertise, rather than raw force, should decide the outcome.

Accordingly, politics is a game. Business is a game. Warfare is a game. And, like it or not, even romance is a game; that is, because romance is not based in real love, romance is, in technical psychological terms, a game, and to play this game you must put yourself in competition with everyone else playing the same game.

In fact, everything within the box of social fraud is a game. Even those persons who can recognize the fraud around them and want to throw a wrench into the works—like political activists—are still playing a game.

There is no escape from fraud and game-playing by playing the game.

There is only one true escape: to step outside the box.

IF you stay within the box, you will be enslaved to the exuberant fantasy that your aching throb of loneliness might be alleviated through someone's body. But outside the box you can be for others a soul enrobed in chaste beauty, and you will be filled with all the fullness of real love.

If you stay within the box, your life will be enslaved to lust and to the manipulation of others for your own pleasure, status, and power. But outside the box you will find the ability to soul for other souls in holiness.

If you stay within the box, your life will be enslaved to pride and to the unremitting defense of your own ego. But outside the box you will find true peace in service to others.

PSYCHOLOGY can teach us, therefore, not only that our social world is a "fraud" but also that it is possible to recognize and heal the pain we feel as children when we experience the world's fraud. It can teach us to speak about those childhood wounds rather than keep them as dark secrets hidden away within ourselves, wrapped in victim anger. It can teach us to let go of bitterness and hatred and to show compassion and love for those secrets, in the hope of healing them, rather than killing them. If those secrets are not healed they become our unconscious enemies—and we become terrorists in a battle against our own pain.

THUS we reach the ultimate irony that your protesting the fraud of the world only makes you part of the fraud.

MAYBE "stress" isn't any "thing" at all. Maybe it's just a descriptive term that our culture uses to normalize unconscious anger, a fear of love, a lack of forgiveness, a desperate clinging to a vain identity, and an absence of a spiritual life. Maybe "stress" is just a convenient myth—a fraud in its own right—to shift responsibility for life away from ourselves and onto something so vague that everyone can love to hate it.

JUST remember that many persons caught up in addictions, such as alcoholism, will, while in a state of intoxication, claim that they are doing nothing harmful to their lives. It's only when they get into a sober state of mind that they can perceive how close to death and total destruction they really were. And so it is in the cultural realm. When you're caught up in all the attractions of the world it's literally impossible to see how close to spiritual ruin you really are.

IT'S not that the television, movies, music, and games of our culture are necessarily evil in themselves—though in some cases they are—but that our attraction to them can draw us away from the good and the peaceful and push us onto the very threshold of the door to malevolence and death.

IN the end, all fantasy literature must encounter its own moral failure. It's just not possible to use glamour and power to convey the deep meaning of humility and self-surrender. And, to be perfectly blunt, a devout religious life grounded in quiet faith and the patient endurance of adversity is, by entertainment standards, simply boring.

AFTER all, what, in all its blindness, does human culture tend to value? Well, look at politics, sports, and entertainment and you will see an insatiable thirst for wealth, glamor, power, competition, and revenge. So is it any wonder that to show us real love, and to bypass all human illusions, God comes to us in poverty, simplicity, weakness, and gentleness?

4 DEPRESSION

To the "Other," you (and all of us, for that matter) are just an object to be manipulated to satisfy someone else. It's a losing game to try to make the "Other" love you. It's a losing game to make the "Other" say you're special. Sure, you can try to do all the right things, like drink the right brand of cola, eat at the right fast-food place, wear the right jeans, expose all the right pieces of flesh, pierce and tattoo yourself in the right places, use the right lingo, work for the right company—but once you slip up, then it's the garbage can for you.

I am not trying to tell you here that nobody feels affection for you. You can argue all you want that your mother and father care about you somehow, and I won't object, because on some level they do care about you. The real point is that many persons who claim to care about you also give indications, through behaviors and things they say and think, that their affection for you is mixed with resentment. Thus, instead of teaching you *how* to love by the *example* of real love, they "infect" you emotionally with a fear of love. It's not pretty to see this directly, so that's why you have defenses that blind you to it. But it's real. At the core, that's where suicidal feelings originate. Not that anyone is necessarily literally wishing you to die, but that the feeling of resentment that they project can get so strong that you end up feeling like garbage. And from there it is only one small step to *make yourself garbage.*

IN depression there is nothing but darkness, yet it is not seen as darkness or recognized as darkness. Blind to divine reality, this darkness seems to be the only reality. *For it is impossible to perceive one's darkness without the divine light focusing on it.*

I have had clients walk into a session saying, "I'm feeling really depressed this week. I'm sure it's biochemical. Maybe I need medication."

When I ask what has happened during the week, they reply with a shrug of the shoulders, "Nothing special. It's just me."

Then I patiently explore with them the events of the week and their emotional reactions to those events. Invariably, we discover some interpersonal conflict that activated old feelings of shame and guilt and that had a direct connection to the depressed mood. At the end of the session they say, "I'm feeling much better. I never would have discovered that connection on my own."

So, were they lying to me at the beginning of the session? Well, no, not in the sense of deliberately telling a lie. But were they lying to themselves? Sadly, yes.

Therefore, I will say it again. Once your psychotherapy

drags you through the pain of this realization about human nature—and you accept it all without defense and resistance—you will then have the strength to "see through" the illusions of the "Other" and claim your own right to exist.

THE irony about depression is that it actually disavows your deepest pain and tries to hide it all with a thick smokescreen of victimization and self-loathing. But if you listen to your pain and vulnerability you give yourself the respect and recognition that you can't get from the world, and you take the first step toward your own healing.

WHY does anger get turned toward the self? It might happen out of a perception that you could have done something to protect yourself from being so vulnerable to loss, and, having failed to do it, you feel deserving of condemnation. It could be that someone from your past treated you like an object for his or her own pleasure and you come to believe that you are nothing but garbage. It could be that the person responsible for the hurt in the first place was someone loved, and it might feel too psychologically risky to feel irritated with such a person. After all, the person might withdraw "love" in retaliation. Or it might happen that the hurt was caused by some trauma or disaster, and, though you might blame God, if you're at all religious, you can't allow yourself to be angry with God—so you blame yourself while secretly hating God.

So there you are, trapped in self-hatred, a lonely victim, stuck in "anger turned inwards," right in the middle of depression.

CONSIDER this fundamental axiom in psychology: *It's nearly impossible for you to change the behavior of anyone other than yourself.*

Children in dysfunctional families, for example, feel the intense urge to want to fix the family, such as by changing the behavior of their father or mother (e.g., stopping one of them from being an alcoholic). But, being children and lacking an understanding of the fundamental axiom in psychology, many of these children will feel frustrated at their failure to fix their parents; having no way to cope with feelings of intense helplessness, they end up blaming themselves—and often blaming God—that they have not been able to stop their father's or mother's irresponsible and self-destructive behavior.

So they grow up to find their lives stained with emotional and interpersonal instability, stained with confusion about their purpose in life, and stained with depression—with unconscious anger at the core of it all.

5 DESPAIR

CONSIDER how you were conceived. How we *all* were conceived. Through the passion of our parents, sperm and egg came together to form a beginning embryo. Notice well: an embryo. To your parents, at your conception, you were not "you." You were not a "special" person. No, nothing of the sort. Whoever you are, whatever you think you are, however you want to be seen in this world—none of this mattered to your parents. All they knew was the passion of their desire.

It may have been the desire for nothing more than the physical pleasure of the moment, of which conception was—to use the terminology of scientific medicine—just a "side effect." Or it may have been the fully-planned desire to have a baby. But, again, note well: a baby. If your parents wanted a baby, they knew—and wanted—nothing of you as a person; they just wanted "a baby."

To the sexual operation which created you, therefore, *you*—despite all your longing for a special identity—are nothing but a remainder.

And herein lies all the desperation that life is heir to, because, once born, each child will spend the remainder of its life hiding this unwanted reality from itself.

We will waste our lives seducing our despair.

EVERY child born into this world is born into a pre-existing social world of language, science, technology, art, literature, and so on. But even more profound than the mystery of the sum total of all this factual information is the mystery of the child's own body. The child finds itself literally at the mercy of biological processes—eating, vomiting, defecation, urination, bleeding, reproduction, and death—that it can neither control nor comprehend. Thus the child will feel excluded and will believe—rightly so—that the world "knows" something that he or she does not know. Right from the beginning, then, the child is located in the unknown surrounded by a profound emotional space of "not knowing" and feeling "left out."

Moreover, when children are criticized and humiliated by others, they can develop the belief that others are deliberately withholding knowledge from them, and this belief can cause the children to burn with anger at their parents in particular and the world in general. Such children can develop an intense desperation to want to figure out everything in advance, before risking doing anything, so as to avoid further feelings of humiliation.

THERE are no social or political organizations you can join, nations to which you can avow citizenship, cultures in which you can take pride, languages you can speak, or identifications in which you can dress yourself that have the power to free you from this shadowy despair.

IT'S an awkward and uncomfortable place to be. And so we all devote considerable energy to overcoming the feeling of "not knowing." We might seek out intellectual knowledge through formal education. We might engage in scientific research. We might join country clubs, gangs, cults, cliques, or any other social organization that purports to offer some secret "knowledge." We might search through myriads of pornographic images hoping for the special privilege of seeing what is usually kept hidden. We might seek out "carnal knowledge" through the body of another person and attempt to locate the psychological agony of our bodily mystery in the pleasure—or pain—of the *other*. Or we might create our own fantasy worlds—with thoughts and images of eroticism, heroism, revenge, or destruction—in which we can "figure it out" on our own so as to possess the power and recognition we so desperately crave.

Nevertheless, all the "knowledge" in the world is nothing but a thin veil that hangs over the dark anguish of helplessly "not knowing." Standing before the veil, suspecting the secret truth of our "not knowing," we feel confused, disgusted, weak, useless, and deceived.

WE humans have language—along with a memory system with which to process it—and trauma has a unique linguistic way of lingering in our unconscious minds. We may give the appearance of being well-adjusted, but, as any experienced mental health clinician has seen over and over, many of the seemingly "well-adjusted" individuals walking around in our society are tormented by inner lives of emptiness and self-destructive despair.

MANY women alcoholics have had abortions at some time in the past, and this secret thorn-in-the-flesh only adds to the woman's guilt and despair, especially if she abandoned her faith in the first place because of her parents' hypocrisy.

THE urge to masturbate begins because you have been feeling helpless, ineffectual, or deprived in some way. It grows in you because of (a) unconscious anger at your parents for not nurturing you with real love and (b) unconscious anger at yourself for feeling so incompetent because of a lack of real love. Now, these feelings of helplessness and deprivation will vary in detail from person to person and from situation to situation, but the point is that instead of turning to God in the midst of your emotional pain, you lose patience, and, in a moment of spite, you give in to the urge to take matters into your own hands to relieve yourself of your own despair. Literally.

SOME person's lives are plagued by stuckness, self-sabotage, and a lack of success. Now, where does this desire for self-destruction "come from"?

Well, consider a woman, newly married to a man who turns out to be irresponsible, and now despairingly pregnant with a child she doesn't want. Right in the womb that developing fetus will be "infected" psychologically with the belief that "It would be better if you were dead."

Or maybe a woman is too emotionally immature to attend to an infant's needs. As that infant struggles with the dark terror of its neglect, it will be "infected" psychologically with the belief that "It would be better if you were dead."

Or maybe the child is a living "accident," the unanticipated result of raw sexual pleasure stripped of any responsibility to reproduction. As that child struggles with lonely isolation, it will be "infected" psychologically with the belief that "It would be better if you were dead."

However it may originate—in the womb, as an infant, throughout childhood—the child's unconscious desire will be to destroy itself in fulfillment of the rejection it feels from its parents. And that desire will persist even into adult despair, where it will wreak its own secret havoc, unless it is recognized and healed.

YOU make a good point about appealing "to those on the fence who might have been told all of their lives that they are garbage." These are today's lost sheep who have wandered off into spiritual wilderness because of family dysfunction. The deceit, the game-playing, and the abuse that have been inflicted on children—by parents, mind you, who claim that sin and hell are old-fashioned up-tight ideas and who have discarded the fear of God—have created generations of poor lost souls, completely lacking in moral guidance, who feel like garbage.

ALL that worry and all that self-blame is rust on our souls that prevents us from getting close to God. It's a self-limiting sort of dynamic that keeps us stuck in our own unconscious despair. For no matter how many times you claim to trust in God, if you say the words only intellectually, without deep love in your heart, those words will do no more to heal your fear than a coat of paint can fix crumbling rust.

WE praise God primarily by recognizing that, however we came into this world, and despite any pain or suffering that ever happened to us, we are ultimately God's creation and that God calls us continually into holiness and away from our sins.

And we praise God by living out this holiness as an example to others, so that they might see us and, desiring to share in our great peace and joy, they might be saved from slavery to their sins as well.

Now, if instead of showing others your inner peace you show them how miserable you are because you can't have what you think you want, you aren't *living* your faith. In fact, you are showing others that you *lack* faith. With real faith you will accept everything that God gives you or does not give you. You will accept it all gratefully, and you will accept it with the understanding that it is given to you precisely for the sake of your spiritual purification, to polish out from your soul all the various stains left in you by your past emotional injuries.

So, accept the fact that God knows exactly what you need and that He will give you what you need and will lead you where He knows you need to go. If you resist, you will be miserable. And what pitiful misery it is, to be miserable even in the presence of all God's gifts. But if you cooperate, you will be plunged into the fullness of the gift of love.

IF your pain were to be thought of as a child within you, then your obsession with death as a means to escape your pain would be like a mother rejecting her own child. What greater sadness than this can there be?

Maybe your mother rejected you, and maybe that is the cause of your despair and sadness.

But God is giving you a gift—the gift of gracefully accepting your helplessness—as the means to find what has been lost and to share in God's joy.

IF you choose to believe it, each of us has a soul that, by the grace of pure, selfless love, is unique. And it does mean something—not to the social world, but to love itself. And so, despite death and despair, we have the choice of rebirth, a new "birth" not structured in vain self-satisfaction but in humble emptiness of self.

THE concept of rebirth has been a part of religion for ages. It even entered into psychology through Carl Jung's research into religion and alchemy. But the problem with Jung's ideas—and with his followers such as Joseph Campbell—is that no matter which path to psychological "rebirth" is pointed out, no matter which myth is laid out on the table with all the other myths, they are all nothing but human signifiers, each one as empty as the one lying next to it.

All these myths make one grave mistake: they hold out

the lie that you can find value in life by seeking it through your own psychology.

NOW, you can experience this process spiritually by giving up the worldly identifications which "glue" your sense of "self" together in an illusory identity; as these bonds crumble, you will crumble into your real despair. And then you will be able to accept God's love, for in emptying yourself of your petty desires you make room for real love, and in being filled with love is your forgiveness and healing.

TO accomplish the work of psychotherapy, however, a person must perform a difficult task that even you don't seem to understand. To heal the belief that you are garbage it is necessary stand directly on the garbage pile of your life and dig down into it with your bare hands. It is necessary to feel the hurt—and the hate encrusted around it—from every wound, raw and bleeding in the depths of your heart. And then, seeing it all, feeling it all, and knowing it all, it is necessary to dissolve that crust of hatred and bitterness in the cleansing waters of God's forgiveness and, in turn, forgive those who have hurt you. This is hard work because it amounts to seeing sin for what it is—in yourself and in others. But it's the only path to the honesty that will lead, in turn, to total trust in God.

TRUE rebirth demands something more than psychology. It demands "death." Death of all self-importance, death of all we "think" we are, death of all pride in our il-

lusory identities. It is the death of all attempts to seduce
your despair.

6   EVIL

In its most general sense, *evil* refers to something that is harmful or destructive. This meaning focuses on the effects of something, not its origin.

The second, more specific—and common—meaning of *evil* refers to the refusal to serve God's will. According to theological tradition, this is what caused the fall of Lucifer, the angel of light, who is now called Satan, or simply "the devil." When he fell, many other angels, now called demons, followed him. Together, all these fallen angels, with Satan as their commander, epitomize evil. Unwilling to submit to God's authority, evil makes self-interest, at the expense of others, into its own god.

Why did God create hell? Some people get stuck on that question and, lacking any real theological wisdom, they decide for themselves that God is "mean" and arbitrary and that they want nothing to do with Him.

The true answer to that question, though, is something of a surprise.

Consider that when God created all things, He gave all creatures free will so that they could participate in love. In other words, those who cannot *refuse* to love aren't really capable *of* love—they're just robots. Real love, after all, is an act of will. Without having free will, we could not love. So, in order to give all of His creation the capacity to love, God gave all of His creation free will.

So, there was Lucifer, an angel with free will. Somehow he decided that he did not want to serve God but rather wanted to serve himself. Maybe—just like many individuals in the world today—he thought something like, "I resent the idea of worshipping this God who created me. I want to be free to wield my power for myself. I want to do what *I* want to do."

Now, God, in the fullness of His love, did not get mad. Instead, He must have said something like, "All right. If you want to be your own king, I will give you a place that you can have all for yourself in the company of those who choose to follow you." So, God created hell and gave it to Satan with the understanding that anyone who wants to reject love for the sake of self-interest is free to go to hell.

The astonishing thing about this transaction is that the creation of hell is an act of God's mercy. Because it is absolutely too horrific to contemplate any place entirely separated from God, Satan received from God a place—hell—that exists within God's love. The flames of hell are the flames of God's love that torment only those who have rejected love.

Furthermore, not being entirely excluded from creation, Satan and his demons have the power of influence over souls in this world. It's perfectly fair—Satan has the free will to tempt us to join him in hell, and we have the free will to accept his seduction or, through faith and love, to reject it.

USING any means that they can—bypassing all rules, all justice, all fairness, all truth—terrorists seek to undermine and destroy all that opposes them. And that is the essence of evil, because evil will stop at nothing to achieve its own satisfaction.

IN the end, holiness is a personal struggle, not a political ideology; nevertheless, as holiness grows in individuals it can be reflected into the world to enlighten the darkness that surrounds it. Still, as holiness grows, it grows side-by-side with all the weeds of evil.

THEREFORE, you are vulnerable to the influence of evil in proportion to the extent that you are influenced by unconscious psychological defenses. These defenses serve essentially to protect your pride and ego in the face of family dysfunction and hypocrisy and, commonly because of your anger at the failures of your father, these defenses often seek the unconscious satisfaction of undermining all authority—including God Himself.

THE easiest opening that evil can follow into your heart is the path opened by hatred in its desire to get revenge for injuries inflicted on you. Because this desire is often unconscious, rather than conscious, especially in regard to childhood traumas, you might even say that you are certain that you don't want revenge on anyone. But unconsciously you do desire revenge—and any of those behaviors that "the devil made me do" are the evidence.

So, do you need an exorcism? Well, actually, you can "exorcise" yourself simply by creating an environment within your "house" that is boring to evil. It's like when a neighbor always comes to your house and helps himself to the soda or beer in your refrigerator. You can put an end to the mooching just by not keeping soda or beer in the fridge.

Therefore, in regard to evil, don't keep "revenge" in your house. That is, purge from your house anything that breeds on the desire to "get even with" others, such as social rudeness and cursing, competitive sports, political arguing, and violent video games. Even though meanness, hostility, and triumph are accepted hook, line, and sinker by our culture, they have no spiritual value and are just breeding grounds for strife and hatred. The same for addictions (smoking, drinking, drugs, gambling, pornography); these things breed revenge because by hurting yourself you ultimately inflict your hatred on society at large.

THINK of chaos and filth as aspects of the demonic, whereas cleanliness and order are aspects of the holy. If you respect your environment as an aspect of a holy life, you will be pained to see dirt and disorder anywhere.

Although your mother was a meticulous housekeeper, she certainly wasn't holy, or she wouldn't have abused you. You know she was a hypocrite, and that angers you. You want to throw her cleanliness back in her face so that you can get the satisfaction of showing her what a fraud she was. Therefore, your allowing dirt to accumulate in your (her) house is the expression of anger. The dirt symbolizes your hatred for her.

But allowing this disorder is like unconsciously punishing God because of the hurt your mother caused you. Nothing will ever be resolved this way. Revenge does not heal anything—it only adds to the dirt. Allow yourself, therefore, to see the dirt—the dirt of your hatred—and then, through prayer, fasting, and forgiveness, clean up the evil mess.

FURTHERMORE, never forget the motto of Satanism: "Do what thou wilt." It's like demonic flypaper, sweet on the surface, but ultimate death once you are careless enough to touch it.

NEVERTHELESS, the urge to do some good even while committing sin leaves you still committing a sin. Choosing a lesser evil, therefore, is still a choosing of evil, and that is, well, evil. Period.

THE battle with evil is clear and present; it is fought not with weapons of destruction, though, but with love.

7 FAMILY

THE real commitment of an indissoluble marriage between a man and a woman for the sake of their natural children is the glue that has held human society together for ages. Altering this concept is like someone remodeling a house who decides that removing a load-bearing wall will give the house more openness—but as soon as the wall is removed, the whole house collapses.

ALL of us have experienced the delight of being fed and protected when we were helpless infants. In fact, if we don't experience it, we die. And the delight of this early infantile experience, which makes no demands on us and leaves us free simply to enjoy it, is at the root of our adult yearnings for a "utopia" in which all of our needs are taken care of effortlessly.

But to function responsibly as an adult, a child must pass beyond this care-free infantile state of dependence. If this task fails, the child will remain neurotically dependent on maternal protection and will be afflicted with doubts and anxieties about assuming personal responsibility in the world. Moreover, the child's talents will either remain buried in fear or will be expressed largely through an unconscious grandiosity. And, in its most severe manifestations, alcoholism and drug addictions can develop in adolescence and adulthood, because all addictions have their roots in a desire to escape the demands of personal responsibilities and return to an idyllic feeling of care-free bliss.

A child will more-or-less trust a nurturing mother. This sort of *natural trust*, though, is a necessary part of mother-infant bonding for the sake of the infant's physical survival.

A psychologically deeper trust—a *symbolic trust*—requires that the child grow to depend on and respect the father, a person different from the mother through whom the child was born; that is, the father is a *different body* and a *different gender* from the mother. The father—and only a father—can therefore teach the child to enter the world and encounter *difference* confidently. But, to be a successful teacher, the father must teach this from the place of his own faith and obedience. In other words, the father must live from his heart by the rules he teaches to his children. In this way the children can learn to trust him through his own integrity. Otherwise, the children will see him for a hypocrite and will disavow—openly or secretly—everything he represents.

Now, considering all of this about the role of a father, look about you and see how many fathers fail miserably in their responsibilities. How many fathers are absent from the family because they were nothing more than sperm donors in a moment of lust? How many fathers are absent from the family because of divorce? How many fathers are absent from the family because their adultery draws them away to another woman? How many fathers are absent from the family because they are emotionally insensitive to their children's needs? How many fathers are absent from the family because they are preoccupied with work or sports? How many fathers are absent from the family because they are preoccupied with their own pride and arrogance? How many fathers are absent from the family because of alcoholism? How many fathers are absent from the family because of illness? How many fathers are absent from the family because a woman decided she didn't need a man to have a child? It can go on and on. And it does.

And the sad thing is that when a father is absent—whether physically or emotionally—his lack causes a lack in the children. Lacking understanding of how the world works, lacking trust in others, and lacking trust in themselves, children—whether they be boys or girls—become lost, insecure, and confused. They lack confidence. They lack real faith. They lack a spiritually meaningful future. They lack life. All because their fathers were lacking.

LOOK at communities in which single mothers are the norm, rather than the exception. What do you see there? A male disrespect for women, low educational performance, social disobedience, violence, drug abuse, prostitution, and a general lack of social opportunity.

CONSIDER, for a moment, the way a dysfunctional father treats his family. Instead of being a good father—sympathetic, loving toward others, compassionate, humble, and always returning a blessing for insult—he will, overtly or subtly, wear down his wife and children with criticism and faultfinding. He will play "mind games" with them, denying their feelings even as he smiles at them.

In his selfishness, he denies his children's reality. That denial will wound the children deeply. But, because the children can't just go find another father, and because they lack the psychological capacity to understand the games that are being played with their minds, the pain will be driven down into their unconscious, forcing them to defend themselves internally and intellectually. They will teach themselves to suppress their true feelings. They will view the world with cynicism. And the residue of that defensiveness will continue even into adulthood to affect all of their interpersonal relationships.

This continuing dynamic will be seen especially in the way these adults now treat their own children.

Maybe you are one of these adults.

IT'S always easiest to medicate the "Identified Patient" and then forget about the rest of the family. It would be far better, and more clinically appropriate, to ask some specific—and painful—questions about how the child's symptoms may be reflecting parental conflicts and family anxiety.

YOU have to look carefully at your own life and stop

blaming others. If you are not satisfied with your life, it's probably because you are not living up to your inner potential or are in one way or another betraying your life values. This can be a hard lesson to learn, but be honest—an adulterous sexual affair, for example, is just a perverted attempt to avoid the real problem: yourself.

ANY attempt to "control" the thoughts or behavior of another person is just an unconscious attempt to control—rather than face up to and heal—your own "ugly" inner life. Until you have made peace with yourself, you will never be able to live in peace with anyone else. *So, in this world, you can't change anyone but yourself.* Then, it can be hoped, your example might influence others to change themselves.

This is how it works in life, and this is how it works in a family.

ALTHOUGH some people claim differently, domestic violence is not so much a political problem rooted in "male domination of women" as it is a psychological problem rooted in an unwillingness to take responsibility for one's own life. Granted, there are some persons—male and female—who are so filled with frustration and anger that they will attack anyone—including children, and pets—without provocation. But just as often there is provocation, and violence becomes a sly family dance. There are even some people so good at subtle provocation that they always come off looking like innocent victims. It's a dirty business overall.

THE beginning of the solution to all family problems is to realize that just as plants can't grow in chalky soil unless you add to the soil whatever is needed to make it healthy, so children—and husbands and wives—can't grow unless you give them whatever support and encouragement they need to become independent and responsible. No one can grow in the "chalky soil" of pre-existing desires and expectations. And what a child or spouse needs might not be what you had expected—or wanted.

CHILDREN need help putting complex emotions into words. By listening carefully to the child's concerns, parents can help the child distinguish *anger* from *fear* from *anxiety* from *vulnerability* from *frustration* from *sadness* and so on. Of course, you, the adult, are perfectly capable of sorting out your own emotions, aren't you? Aren't you?

LACKING touch and emotional spontaneity in their families, many children don't even know how to recognize their own emotional experiences. They repress their emotions, they suffer psychosomatic illnesses, and they confuse a need for simple physical affection with sexual desire.

BECAUSE many parents do not live out in their *actions* whatever religious faith they profess with their *lips*, normal family life is more often than not characterized by self-indulgence, resentment, manipulation, hidden alliances, and a general lack of honest communication.

This lack of communication can take either of two

courses. Authority in some families can be a fraud, just an excuse for manipulation or intimidation. This leaves children feeling exasperated and smoldering with anger.

On the other hand, if parents give children too much freedom, the children will grow up without any sense of compassionate discipline and guidance. Most kids are smart enough to realize that when parents give them too much freedom it really means that the parents don't care— or don't know any better themselves. So the children can end up with such profound emptiness and guilt about the meaningless pursuit of self-gratification that they challenge everything out of pure frustration. And where does that lead? To bitter identity confusion, fear, anger, and depression.

In either case, then, a meaningful basis for rules and regulations is never communicated.

QUITE often men are socialized to be aggressive and hostile in their communication, but when women try to attain "equity" with men through aggression and hostility, it only makes matters worse, not better, because then all communication degenerates into endless arguments and rebuttals, and the underlying emotions get trampled underfoot on the battleground.

AS strange as it might seem, a permissive parent who fails to administer discipline actually causes a child to fear punishment and to associate it with irrational violence. These fears can become so strong that the child actually engages in violence as an unconscious plea to be punished for an unspoken, aching sense of guilt for other acts that were never justly punished.

PARENTS who become overly protective of a child after a tragedy only instill a sense of paranoia in the child. If a child is kidnapped in your city, bolting the doors, keeping the drapes closed, and refusing to let your child out of the house only cause additional trauma in your child.

BAD things happen, yes, but far more good things happen each day. Thousands of airplanes take off and land every day without incident. Hundreds of millions of children go about their lives every day without getting hit by cars, abducted, or shot at. Teach your child to trust in the good, not to fear the bad.

"WHY do bad things happen?" Parents often freeze when a child asks this question—or they offer a cynical answer that reflects their own bitterness. Here's the best and simplest answer of all: *God is love, and God created the world to share that love with us. But love can't be commanded; if we are to love, we must love by our own free will, and that means we must have the capacity to not love. Therefore, God gave us free will, and with it came the freedom both to love and also to reject love and do evil. So the more you see evil around you, the more you should be reminded to love from your own heart.*

WHEN seeking out my help in the face of some sort of family crisis, parents often admit to me that they have hid-

den the truth from their children. Then they quickly add,
"I was trying to protect them."

Well, you cannot protect children by hiding anything
from them. You can protect them only by teaching them
to trust in God's protection.

THE adolescent process can be relatively easy and
smooth if parents learn how to communicate effectively
with their children right from the beginning. After all, if
parents are sufficiently committed to their own moral beliefs—if they have any—they can encourage their children
to learn about and discuss those beliefs as they grow up,
and there won't be so much for the children to challenge
in adolescence.

WHEN parents surrender their moral authority to the
popular culture around them, they allow their children to
be brainwashed with popular ideology, and families dis-
integrate into moral indifference and corruption—and
the children are left with gaping emotional wounds of unconscious confusion and anger, social disobedience, and a
crippling lack of faith.

SADLY enough, most adolescent "acting out" derives from
the fact that many parents' values aren't really grounded in a
deep devotion to something greater than themselves, such
as religious faith. So the adolescent in effect says, "Your
values are all a fraud. They're arbitrary. So why should I
do what you say? It's not fair. I'll do what I want because
my desires are just as valid as any of yours."

SIMPLY stated, adolescents feel worthless because their parents' lives are valueless—that is, without meaningful, spiritual values. And communication fails because the family is governed by a fear of love.

In a similar way, much of adolescent "acting out" (which technically means communicating behaviorally rather than verbally) is an unconscious attempt to prove to the parents that they are full of you-know-what.

IT'S a great sadness that most parents do not teach their children how to love. Love is hard work, and most parents shrink from that work. When children do something wrong, for example, it's far easier to tell the children they will go to hell if they misbehave than to show them consistently, by example, that all behavior should be inspired by love for God. And so the children grow up being afraid of hell and understanding nothing about real love.

IT'S a very sad thing. Family emotional wounds can leave children believing that God is cruel, that God is unfair, that God plays games with us, and that they have no other recourse than to take matters into their own hands to get what they *think* is right. But God is not unfair. God is just. It's families who have lost their grounding in faith that are cruel and unfair and have turned interpersonal relationships into game playing.

WHEN children aren't taught the "language" of honest emotional encounter within their families, children tend to seek out "natural" ways—that is, physical, bodily ways—to derive attention and satisfaction from the world, such as through food, drugs, or sexuality. So we have a world filled with addictions, eating disorders, and sexual perversions.

IT all starts when parents fail to raise children in an atmosphere of devout holiness, and fail to teach them to love and to fear God—that is, to hold God in awe—and to trust always in His guidance and protection. Lacking clear guidance—and often suffering outright abuse—the children become conflicted about faith itself. They might accept "faith" intellectually, but it means nothing to them in any practical sense. Instead of learning to revere and trust in God, children inadvertently learn, through parental game-playing and manipulation, to seize whatever satisfaction they can get from the world.

And so, claiming to value peace and love, your parents actually sought out pride, self-advancement, and aggression. In the midst of this hypocrisy, then, and in your failure to learn to trust in an unseen God, you essentially learned to believe only in what you can see. Instead of taking God seriously, you end up taking God for granted.

8 FEAR

ANYTHING done out of real love is a virtue, but anything done out of fear has the character of a mental disorder.

NOTE here that someone who pays close attention to details out of love for the work at hand acts virtuously, whereas someone who obsesses about details out of fear that something bad might happen if everything is not done perfectly acts with the characteristics of Obsessive-Compulsive Disorder (OCD).

NOW, some practitioners of psychology—especially those under the influence of managed care—will do nothing but fix "broken bones." But if you are willing to get to the cause of the problem, and if your psychologist knows his or her job, then it is inevitable that you will encounter in the psychotherapy the deep secrets and dark, ugly terrors of your psyche. In fact, a client once said to me that the truth is not just ugly but is "worse than humiliating."

At this point the whole psychotherapy is put to the test. Many clients will run from psychotherapy in fear and terminate prematurely. But the real challenge at this point is *to explore in the psychotherapy the very reasons for being afraid of it.*

CHILDREN who have dysfunctional parents learn from experience that if they express any of their needs, they will be punished or rejected by their parents. After all, some so-called "parents" are incompetent as parents because they lack the responsibility to be physical and emotional caretakers of children, most likely because they themselves were abused by their own "parents."

Caught in the middle of this mess, then, children will learn to fear rejection and criticism and will conclude that denying their needs—holding them back, as it were—will prevent their being rejected.

So, as soon as a dream materializes, BANG! they shoot it down before it has a chance to get off the ground.

These are the persons who say, "I don't know" when asked what they want. These are the persons who say, "I don't know" when asked what they feel. These are also the same persons who will say, "It isn't fair! God hates me! Whenever I try to do anything, it never works out!"

But God doesn't hate them; they hate themselves—they condemn themselves, they punish themselves, they sabotage themselves—in *fear* of having dreams.

CHILDREN of alcoholic parents more often than not grow up in an environment of lying, broken promises, arguing, and violence. To cope with such emotional volatility and chaos, some children learn to run away and hide.

They fear emotions as something dangerous. And, because the dysfunctional family system cheats them of the ability to deal honestly with emotions, the children spend their lives avoiding emotions, knowing that if they ever encountered a strong emotion, they wouldn't know what to do with it.

FAMILIES are often taken by surprise at how easily and quickly attempts at honest communication can fall into misperceptions and angry rebuttals.

Actually, this is a common problem, and it happens to one extent or another in most families. Despite the parents' best attempts to protect and discipline a child, there can be elements in the parents' words and behavior that leave the child feeling misunderstood and criticized. With no one to correct the miscommunication, the parents will become more and more frustrated, the child will become more and more hurt and angry, and a huge emotional rift will separate the family.

The child, in feeling hurt, alone, and frightened, will do and say things to express disappointment, but the parents will find the child's behavior disrespectful, will get offended, and will say, "This deserves the belt!"

Therefore, the strongest and wisest member of the family could be of greatest help just by not taking the child's behavior personally. Rather than respond with indignation at what a child says or does, a parent needs to think, "This is the way she is expressing her hurt and fear. It's a plea for help. She needs comfort, encouragement, and protection, not criticism or punishment."

When a child seems hostile, a parent can non-threateningly remind her that her communication has gotten off track and that the parent is willing to help her express herself more honestly. But if the parent takes the child's behavior as a personal offense and reacts defensively and critically, it will only provoke the child into more of her own hostility.

WHY are there so many lives headed for the garbage dump? Fear. Fear of the hard work of going to psychotherapy to clean themselves off. Fear of letting go of the dirt. Dirt is all they know, and, even if it's dirt, at least it's comfortable.

FEAR keeps alcoholics drinking, addicts addicted, and wretched sinners stuck in sin like quicksand. In fearing the darkness of the human psyche you never get to feel the true joy of real light, because, after all, the light of truth illuminates the dark and shows the darkness for what it is. So there you are, in full irony: in your fear of the dark, you end up fearing love itself.

I have had clients—some in residential or day treatment settings, some temporarily in hospital settings—confide to me, "The people here are crazy, and I'm not talking about the patients."

Because I have worked in most mental health settings—crisis, inpatient, outpatient, and residential—at one time or another during the course of my training, and because I have seen with my own eyes the same things my clients complain of, I can acknowledge an unpleasant fact of the mental health system: there are counselors, nurses, and doctors who make mistakes and won't admit it, who don't keep promises, who lie to clients, and who are even afraid of their clients.

THREATS of hell mean nothing to those who do not love God.

Why is this? Well, such persons have been so miserably treated in childhood, and feel so much anger and resentment at how they were treated, that when they feel hurt and wounded as adults they seek out the only comfort they know: sin. And in persisting in sin, they reveal their real fear: the fear of love.

So, in the end, the fear of hell won't save you from hell because it's the fear of love that condemns you to hell.

WHAT is it everyone fears? We're all afraid that if we really change our lives and witness the truth, our families will reject us. We're afraid that our husbands or wives will divorce us and we will lose a nice, comfortable life. We're afraid that our co-workers and friends will criticize us. We're afraid that our social prestige will suffer. We're afraid that our careers will be threatened. In short, *we're afraid of what we might lose.*

And, in being afraid of what we might lose, we place ourselves at risk of losing everything nevertheless.

EVERY child will suffer some form of emotional misunderstanding in his or her family. If this misunderstanding is damaging enough—for example, if the parents are emotionally distant, hypocritical, or abusive—the child can adopt either of two variations of a powerful defensive belief:

"I don't *deserve* to be cared for."

"It's *wrong* to want anyone to care for me."

With these beliefs in place, the child effectively pushes love out of his or her life. Left unhealed, these beliefs will remain in the unconscious even into adulthood. Fear of love will persist, and God Himself—who *is* love—will be pushed away as well.

THE core of any addiction involving intoxication or euphoria is your feeling so deprived of your primal desire—real love from your parents, especially through the lack of your father—and so angry about it, that you use the addiction to hide (i.e., deny) the "stain" of the anger. Thus you settle for any satisfaction of intense excitement—and then, because the intensity of the satisfaction is, according to its own materialism, short-lived, you crave it more and more, over and over. All of this is an unconscious way to avoid giving to others the real love that, despite your craving for it, you secretly fear.

WHEN faced with any new task, (a) remind yourself that you fear the unknown and doubt yourself because your father failed to provide you with comfort and motivation and that his failures have crippled you; (b) in spite of your doubts, call upon the hope of knowing real guidance and comfort in a way you have never known before;

and (c) offer your true successes and achievements from now on to God, for use in His service, and also as a special gift to your father in the hope that someday his eyes, too, might be opened.

WHEN we make the decision to commit ourselves to love, we, by definition, set aside all acts of revenge, both in regard to others and in regard to ourselves. This is an absolute decision; when our lives are governed by a commitment to learn and grow from our mistakes, we are freed from being stuck in fear.

9   FORGIVENESS

TO forgive someone means that you consciously make the decision to set aside any desire to see a person hurt because of the hurt he or she caused you, and instead you wish that the person will recognize his or her hurtful behavior, feel sorrow for it, and learn to be a more considerate person.

I have seen individuals, for example, who have lost a family member because of a crime. The survivors' anger and desire for revenge poison their entire beings. They so focus on what they've lost, and what they wanted the dead person to *be*, and *do*, for *them*, that they completely miss the opportunity they've been given to learn about real love.

Instead, they seem to believe that hatred, even to the point of capital punishment, will satisfy their thirst for vengeance and will somehow bring them healing.

So, with hardened hearts and stiff lips, they say, "I'll never forgive."

And the sad thing is that in wishing to send someone to hell they end up sending themselves there as well.

Think about that.

IN effect, to tell someone to go to hell—no matter what language you say it in—is to send yourself there as well.

SEEKING revenge or wishing harm to another will, at the minimum, deplete your strength and prevent your wounds from healing. In the worst case, the cold hunger for revenge will make you into a victimizer yourself. Lacking forgiveness, you and your victimizer will be locked together in the hell of eternal revenge.

PUSHING the pain into your unconscious only makes forgiveness impossible because, as unconscious anger, the dark wish to harm the person who hurt you remains alive but out of sight.

Then, with your animosity kept out of sight, it's all too easy to present yourself as a "nice" person when, deep inside, you really remain an angry victim.

IN order to live honestly and take full responsibility for your own life, you have to learn in psychotherapy to put your hurt and anger onto the "table" in front of you so you can examine your emotions consciously. And then, when it has been brought to the surface and acknowledged, it can be swept away in forgiveness. Until this work has been done thoroughly, however, the statement "I am a forgiving person" is just an illusion.

The illusion is shown for what it is when many unsuspecting persons say, "OK. I've talked about my traumas. I've forgiven everyone. It's all on the table. But I'm still miserable. What's wrong?" It's as if, after having made what seems to be a simple act of forgiveness, they walk past that "table" and say, "What's that odd smell?" And then, as they look more closely, and admit to all the things they have been hiding from themselves, they find an ugly, moldy mass of unconscious anger that has been growing secretly underneath the table. So that, too, has to be examined.

A common problem with persons caught up in unconscious anger at their parents is that they will try to deny their unpleasant feelings by saying, "But my parents tried their best to be good parents. I have no right to be angry with them."

The truth, however, is that even parents who do their best always cause some emotional hurt to their children, even if it's unintentional. Even if your best friend steps on your foot, it still hurts, right? The therapeutic task is to admit all of your childhood hurt, not to blame your parents, but to allow the light of honesty to heal the wounds.

Ironically, then, in finally admitting all that anyone has done to hurt you, in recognizing what you are really feeling, and in then being able to forgive that person—of everything—you discover real love.

ALTHOUGH some persons are truly selfish and inconsiderate, sometimes a person is simply distracted or confused, not maliciously trying to get in your way. Looking at the "other side" is called empathy, and it can go a long way to calming yourself down, keeping the peace, and fostering simple courtesy.

THE popular advice to "forgive and forget" completely misses the point. Forgetting, in psychological language, is called *repression*. When something is repressed, it just lingers in the dark shadows of the unconscious, along with all the emotions associated with it. And as long as those emotions, such as anger, are brewing secretly in the unconscious, genuine forgiveness remains impossible.

WHEN you speak about the fact that "forgiving" others is easier than forgiving ourselves, you expose the psychological deception of "premature forgiveness." Premature forgiveness isn't really forgiveness at all; that's why it's so easy. It's just a way to distract ourselves from our own pain by saying the politically correct words and doing the politically correct things as a pretense that we love others, when really our hearts are swollen with unspoken bitterness for what we have lost. It's just an intellectual way of telling ourselves that everything is fine when really we haven't felt the pain and brought it to God in heartfelt scrutiny and prayer.

LET us be careful here to understand a fundamental point about forgiveness: Acknowledging and feeling the emotional hurt that you have suffered is a prerequisite to forgiveness. Hiding your feelings only drives them into the unconscious where they fester in unconscious anger, making forgiveness impossible.

Therefore, only when you have felt your pain, are honest with yourself about it, and have understood it psychologically and spiritually, can you make the conscious decision—that is, as an act of will—to lay down your weapons of revenge and then trust in God's justice.

ALL of this points to two facts about the psychology of forgiveness: if you cannot let go of your desire for vengeance, you will never find true healing, and you can never be truly healed if you try to force someone else to pay for the cost of your healing.

TO love is to be giving, and to be giving is to act with patience, kindness, mercy, compassion, understanding, and, ultimately, forgiveness. Activists, by definition, don't love—they demand. In fact, those who clamor the loudest for tolerance often react with hostile intolerance of anyone who disagrees with their agenda.

FORGIVENESS is one thing—it means that God won't push you away for making mistakes if you turn back to Him in sorrow. But you still have to "pay" for the evil that you have brought into the world through your behavior.

The best penance to pay for that mistake now, before you die, is to spread the seeds of spiritual fruit. It's similar to alms giving, which is a traditional penance. Just as giving alms requires a giving of money from your resources, spreading the seeds of your spiritual fruit is also a giving of yourself. Without arrogance and pride holding you back, you can start to produce spiritual fruit, and the seeds that you spread—that is, the holy influence you have on others—is a fitting penance for having previously stifled your spiritual development—and for cheating others of the good you could have done for them.

So remember that if anyone has ever hurt you, you don't *find* forgiveness, you *give* it.

If you have ever hurt others, all you can do is feel sorrow for your behavior; in sorrow, you can apologize, and you can make amends, but whether or not others forgive you is their choice.

And if you have hurt yourself? Well, it's a self-deception to believe that you can forgive yourself. Even though self-destructive and self-sabotaging behavior may seem to be anger at the self, at its core it is an expression of anger at someone else, because of what that person did *to* you or failed to do *for* you. It's as if you amplify the effects of the original injury and throw your dysfunction back into the face of the one who hurt you, in an attempt to force him to see how much he hurt you. It may be unpleasant to admit it, but, in all truth, you use your disability unconsciously as a subtle form of revenge, which is itself a form of hate. For the original wound to heal, you must set aside your personal desire for satisfaction, and forgive, not yourself, but the person who hurt you in the first place.

Speaking of letting go of anger at your father—begin to discharge the static buildup of desiring the satisfaction of "hurting your father as he has hurt you." This sort of satisfaction is called *revenge*; it traps you in blame, and it is revealed for what it is when the grace of God cures your psychological blindness and you see that all your failures have had one secret intent: to hurt your father.

Your true success now will depend on giving up the satisfaction of hurting your father, and you can do this by pursuing real achievement for the love of God. Up until now you have been unconsciously seeking failure so as to punish your father; now you can seek achievement to exalt God the Father. This "discharge" is called forgiveness because it is the cessation of your secret hatred for your father and the beginning of genuine love for God and for all.

"WHAT about national defense?" you might ask. "How can forgiveness and the need for self-defense be reconciled?" Well, I'm not about to try to tinker with national defense strategy, whether through commentary or through protest. Psychology concerns the individual, and forgiveness is an individual act. And for that matter, peace is also a matter of individual will, not of politics. No government can order you to love, and no government can order you to hate. So ultimately you have to live—and die—with the destiny of your own conscience.

THE religious concept of "praying for your enemies" can therefore be expressed psychologically as simply hoping that the person who injured you will ultimately recognize his or her destructive behavior and repent it—as opposed to your wishing for that person's destruction. Saint Teresa of Avila once had a vision of hell; the place was so horrifying, she said, that she wouldn't wish it on her worst enemies. Think about that.

10 GUILT

ONE very common lack in contemporary families is the failure to treat children with unconditional nurturing guidance and protection. So instead of learning real love in their families, children—through all sorts of family manipulation and game-playing, if not outright abuse—are essentially taught to fear love. Moreover, the pain of all this loneliness, guilt, and fear will live on in the unconscious, in a sort of timeless emotional imprisonment, even as the child grows through childhood and adolescence to adulthood.

IMAGINE how it feels to be a child whose parents are abusive, critical, neglectful, and manipulative. These parents not only break down their child into a pile of sticks, but also, when the child stands there covered in guilt and shame, they tell the child, "Look at you! You're just a piece of garbage."

CHILD abuse always provokes feelings of hurt and insult in the child, and almost inevitably that hurt leads to a feeling of hate and a desire for revenge. In fact, even many ordinary, non-abusive frustrations of childhood will provoke feelings of hurt and anger. But because children are not usually taught to express hostile feelings in any healthy way (and because they aren't taught the psychological meaning of anger, and because they aren't taught the psychological meaning of forgiveness and reparation), children quickly learn, through fear and guilt, to hide their true feelings from their parents.

GUILT results from childhood psychological wounds of family dysfunction. Parents all too often fear real love themselves and shrink from the work it takes to teach their children real love. So the parents resort to using guilt to control their children, constantly threatening the children with the fear of punishment in hell. Thus, for the children, it essentially means that whenever you have done (or felt or thought) something "bad" you don't want to admit it or seek help because you are terrified of the irrational family cruelty that will be inflicted on you if anyone discovers your secret. And so you do anything to hide from discovery, while your secret festers in the dark depths of your heart. Moreover, in this forlorn state, you are far removed from real love because all the good you do for others is motivated unconsciously by the desire to appease others to keep them from abandoning you.

IN your inability to understand just why your parents were so mean, you came to believe that something must really be wrong with you and that you really did deserve such abuse. Thus you cultivated a secret shame—and guilt—yearning to be punished *for being defective.* Second, you became so terrified of your anger at your parents for their mistreatment of you that you secretly desired to be punished *for your anger.* Call it a sort of double masochistic whammy.

AND then, on top of all this self-punishing behavior, as a further way to absolve themselves from guilt, children take on the false belief that they are responsible for the feelings of those who injured them in the first place! Thus they end up trying to protect the very persons who are (or have been) injuring them. Eventually, they will hear themselves saying irrational things such as, "But I can't leave him! He needs me!"

AS a result of psychotherapy, he could recall the rest of the story. His mother had denied him something he wanted (though what it was is long forgotten), he felt unrecognized and unloved, and he was angry at her. In his mind, he began to wish she were dead—but only for a split second, because on the edge of consciousness it occurred to him that if she were to die, he would have no mother and that he would be left all alone in the world with no one to take care of him. So his mind quickly turned away from that wish for her death, with all of it's lonely implications, and, feeling quite guilty about the whole thing, he began to wish for his own death. After all, what kind of a person could be so dependent on someone else, so helpless and afraid? A no good piece of nothing, that's who, and he deserves to die.

PSYCHOLOGICAL research into early infant develop-ment has shown that experiences of rage, and subsequent feelings of guilt, happen to us all right from early infan-cy. Every parent will make mistakes in empathic bonding with a child, and every child will feel emotionally hurt by those mistakes and will crave the satisfaction of revenge: to hurt the other "as I have been hurt."

Most children manage to work through this guilt in-tuitively and have no lasting problems from it. Some chil-dren, however, because of subtle, guilt-producing family dynamics, will grow up lacking a social structure of deep faith and trust in God's mercy, and will feel so guilty about having this desire for revenge that they try to hide it from others—and from themselves.

Moreover, these children will more likely than not also find that puberty becomes a troubling time. Lacking clear and honest explanations of sexuality, and lacking guidance about and protection from sexual feelings, budding ado-lescents can develop obsessive and agonizing guilt about their sexuality.

Therefore, both psychological theory and clinical prac-tice lead us to the understanding that Obsessive Compul-sive Disorder (OCD), at its core, is a neurotic way of cop-ing with feelings of guilt. It's similar to Lady Macbeth, in Shakespeare's play *Macbeth*, crying, "Out, damned spot!" as she tries compulsively to rub the stain of Duncan's mur-der from her hands.

CHILDREN feel *shame* because of the injury of feeling unloved, but, even worse, children feel *guilt* because of the inevitable thoughts and fantasies that signify the anger ("I hate you!" "I wish you were dead!").

NOTE that whereas *shame* derives from a belief that there is something "wrong" with you for having certain feelings (such as feeling unloved), *guilt* derives from something you have done or thought (such as thoughts of hatred).

TO heal those old wounds of abuse, though, as an adult you must look back with sorrow—not guilt—on all of your failures to speak up as a child. Acknowledge the pain, and the sadness, and the fear—and the anger—of not having the protection and guidance your parents should have provided for you. Realize that, if they had provided proper guidance, you would have learned how to defend yourself appropriately. Then do all it takes, now, to learn to speak with honesty and integrity in the present.

FROM what you have told me, I suspect that your writer's block derived from unconscious anger at your mother. I have seen, from my own clinical experience, that writer's block tends to result from some current pressure to be productive; it can be as if you are being forced to make your words speak "lies" rather than let them speak their own truth. This pressure can build to such a frustratingly intense creative blockage because unconsciously you are re-experiencing the frustration from your childhood when your own mother pressured you in one way or another. Back then, the anger was so intense—and led to such guilt—that you had to suppress it. Now, as an adult writer, the pressure to produce (even if it may be self-induced pressure) rekindles that old anger. In this sense, writer's block is analogous to apathy, a particular form of anger that leaves you unable even to speak.

BUT—and here is the problem—some part of you resists openly acknowledging those impulses of anger, so you experience a conflict of wanting to care for your mother and fix her versus wanting to hurt her. Moreover, this conflict pains you with guilt, so you end up punishing yourself for your impulses to anger.

NOW, the point here is not to give you an excuse to dodge responsibility for your own actions. We all do and say things that hurt others, and when we are called to correction, we should accept the rebuke honestly and non-defensively. But a rebuke is no reason for feeling depressed. If you do feel depressed, then you have good evidence that the present rebuke has activated unconscious shame and guilt. To deal with the present situation, then, turn back to remedying the emotional wounds of your childhood.

GRANTED, it can take a lot of training and experience to notice the subtle cues a client gives when avoiding emotions, so if your psychotherapist isn't up to the job, you might want to find someone who's better suited to help you. Of course, given your problems with intimacy, you probably feel a certain allegiance to your psychotherapy, even as it is failing you. Remember, that's how you felt about your mother, right? Instead of speaking the truth about how she failed you, you reject your true feelings and make yourself feel guilty for having those feelings. Now it will be important, in order to put your past to rest and to free your future from inhibition, to desire the courage to face your unconscious truth.

To do the job well, though, the psychotherapist must be willing and able to probe into all the dark and unpleasant areas of your psyche that you, in shame and guilt, would prefer to keep hidden.

I think your psychotherapist needs her own psychotherapy. She is actually treating you the way some parents treat their children: unable to accept responsibility for their own behavior, they unconsciously make the children feel shame and guilt, and so the children spend the rest of their lives believing something is wrong with them.

These guilt-inducing thoughts and fantasies are commonly warded off in one of two ways:

1. *Turning them inward.* You say self-negating things to yourself ("I don't deserve to be loved," or "I don't deserve to be here," or "I don't deserve to be alive"), which results in depression.

2. *Trying to neutralize them.* You attempt to keep your guilt secret and to resolve it through your

own superstitious efforts, which results in obsessive-compulsive behaviors.

FEELING so guilty for the effects of your anger, you remain tangled in a dysfunctional relationship because you
believe that the other person needs you.

THE dreams could be an admonition, based in guilt.
Imagine, for example, that you are embezzling the bank
for which you work. Then you start having dreams about
burglars breaking into your home. Well, the dreams are
simply a depiction of something happening to you that is
similar to the hurt or moral injury you are inflicting on
someone else. This same dynamic often occurs in children's nightmares: in waking life, children often experience angry feelings toward their parents and yet lack the
cognitive capacity to express these feelings openly; so,
in unconscious guilt, the anger becomes turned against
themselves as threatening nightmare images.

UNCONSCIOUS anger at a father can manifest psychologically as a delusion of persecution—that is, the person believes he is being persecuted by others but is really
being persecuted by his own guilt about his anger at his father. Ironically, the feeling of being persecuted allows the
person to believe he is "special," in compensation for the
humiliation caused by the father's abuse.

11   HATE

THE spiritually negative emotion of *hate* does not necessarily mean a passionate loathing; it can just as well be a quiet, secret desire for harm to come upon someone or something. Hate can be a subtle thing, therefore, and it often is experienced more unconsciously than consciously. Consequently, it will often be very easy to deny that you have any hatred for anyone at all.

WHETHER your dysfunction be extreme—such as suicide, drug addiction, alcoholism, and personality disorders—or more subtle—such as perfectionism, chronic procrastination, or a lack of success in a career—it all has an unconscious intent of hating and hurting your parents (especially your father in regard to his lack of guidance, protection, or emotional involvement) by hating and hurting yourself. And, because this intent is unconscious, it can be maintained right into adulthood—even after your parents have died!

TRYING to change the behavior of others will only cause stress, along with physiological complications such as high blood pressure, when others refuse to do what you want them to do. Moreover, the obstinacy of others will be a wound to your pride, and that can drive you right into the snares of hatred and spiritual murder.

WHEN you fight fire with fire you run the risk of getting burned yourself. So make no mistake here. If the powers of evil cannot destroy you directly with an attack, they will try to make you destroy *yourself* through your own sins of hatred and hostility that you employ in retaliation for having been attacked.

ANY desire for harm to come to another person—whether through active loathing or through passive resentment—is, in its spiritual essence, an evil desire to remove the fullness of life (with its possibility of love and forgiveness) from that person. That's why hatred is spiritually equivalent to murder.

JUST as those who, out of hatred, defile love by committing acts of terror, so anyone who hates those who commit political terror also defiles love. Once you let evil infect your heart with hatred you are one step closer to letting evil possess your soul as well.

IT'S just a shame that so many persons, even many who call themselves religious, who haven't learned their psychological lessons about loving—and praying for and forgiving—their enemies, rather than hating them, become terrorists in their own hearts, in their own communities, and, ultimately, in the world at large.

AND right there you have the psychological truth about our culture: *It's far easier to cast blame in the moment to satisfy our thirst for revenge than it is to address the real problem.*

The killer to truly fear is the killer in your own heart.

Now, you might say, "That's ridiculous. I would never kill innocent people like that [expletive deleted] did!"

Well, think again, because you still have a lot to learn about the psychology of the unconscious. Our entire culture has oriented itself around power and retaliation as a response to fear and vulnerability, and every individual in the culture carries that infection deep within the unconscious. Look carefully at yourself. Hurling curses at someone is an act of hatred, and hatred, in its ugly truth, is psychological murder no less destructive than the murder committed by a teenager with an assault rifle.

Far better to banish hatred from our lives. But we cannot do that the easy way by making hatred illegal, because that only opens the door to hating those who hate. Instead, we must endeavor to purge hatred from our hearts and learn forgiveness.

The enemy is us. Will we learn?

12   HEALING

MANY persons enter psychotherapy hoping to get rid of pain. Some people even manage to use psychotherapy to hide from their emotional pain. But a good psychotherapist won't let you hide from your past or your future, and you will be encouraged to take up the "cup" of your destiny, however much you might wish it would pass from you.

NO unconscious problem deserves to be gotten rid of. All problems need to be treated with compassion and respect. In fact, the part of you caught up in today's problem probably served to keep you alive in the past. Once you come to terms with its unconscious "message" it can quietly retire, or it can find a new, healthy protective role in your life. But if it is "killed off" its wisdom is lost with it.

UNLIKE medical surgery, psychotherapy must be performed without anesthetics. You have to be aware of the process, you have to feel the pain, and you have to look directly at the "ugly" gore inside of you. It's no wonder that most people are afraid of it all.

You will find many claims out there for an easy way to achieve physical and mental healing. But I predict that if you follow such a path—a path not grounded in discipline and hard work—you are likely not to find anything more than self-indulgence. True, one part of you might find something resembling health, but other parts will remain unhealed, angry and fearful. The only escape from the darkness of the easy way is to seek the light and pay the price of genuine healing.

THIS astonishing transformation is open to anyone. Lives of pain and trauma, bitterness and hatred, emptiness and despair—lives that, despite free will, are enslaved to psychological and spiritual blindness—can be healed and transformed.

But please let's understand right from the beginning that spiritual-psychological healing is hard work. It requires discipline. It's tedious. It's frightening. It requires constant effort to monitor your feelings and the impulses that arise with your feelings, and to override those impulses—those signs of what you want personally—with a firm decision to live a holy lifestyle by doing God's will. It's all far easier to serve evil by doing whatever you want.

PSYCHOTHERAPY should be serious business. It shouldn't be about "getting rid" of problems; it should be about making peace with your problems, taking responsibility for your life—even if you didn't ask for it—disentangling yourself from the desires of the world around you, and discovering something about a human potential you didn't even know you had. But you have to want psychotherapy as much as you want to breathe.

PEACE of mind—or mental health—doesn't come from physical practices. Nor can you "buy" it. You can pay a shaman to adjust your energy fields, you can wear crystals, and you can fill your house with all the aromatherapy scents in the world, but it won't heal you of the inner anger and loneliness that torment you. These unconscious wounds can be healed only by facing up to their origins and making peace with them.

JUST as the "dark night of the soul" strips away all human illusion and pretension, so psychotherapy must strip away everything that hides the deepest ugliness in our hearts. For only by recognizing the perversion in his or her own heart can the individual then recognize the sin that stains all of humanity. And in that community of universal sinfulness will grow the seed of compassion and real love.

POLITICS is an adversarial system in which individuals obstruct their opponents' goals with the hope of eliminating the opponents altogether. Psychology, however, must be based in the hope of making peace with your internal "enemies" so as to find healing; it's not about "getting rid" of pain or blaming others. Therefore, nothing in psychology needs to be expressed in political terms because psychology is about helping you find out what you want to do, not about telling you what to do. Or, to say it another way, whereas politics tries to dictate the behavior of others, psychology helps you willingly change your own behavior.

So remember that it's simply not possible to use blame, hatred, and aggression to make someone else—or your-self—act with kindness. And for that very reason, "po-litical correctness" has no place in the consultation office. There's room only for three persons: you, your psycho-therapist, and the unconscious.

THE task of teaching the general public the difference between happiness and mental health has all the satisfac-tion of trying to fill a sieve with water. And yet, to para-phrase Saint Francis of Assisi, if we accept the world's in-justice, cruelty, and contempt with patience, without be-ing ruffled, and without murmuring, then we have found the path to perfect joy.

YOU have to promise to remedy your lack. Note that this is not a promise that you will "never do such a thing again," because that would be a wild promise that could easily be broken. No, you must go deeper; you must promise that you will do whatever it takes to get to the roots of the be-havior itself and alter things for the better.

YOU *can't bring the dead back to life. You can't change the past.* These are both true and accurate psychological state-ments. But with true sorrow you can learn from the past and change your behavior in the present so that you don't "kill" again. No matter how bad the mistakes you have made in the past, the heaviest penalty you can pay for all that damage is to make a true psychological change and dedicate yourself to learning from those mistakes and doing good from now on.

TRUE healing involves two things: (a) to see clearly what is wrong and (b) to have the compassion to call it to change. This means, first of all, that unconditional acceptance of anything gets you nowhere. If you take no responsibility for the world around you, and if you're unwilling to call error for what it is—that is, if you're always missing the point—then you contribute nothing of any healing value to the world. And that's not love. On the other hand, if you treat error with hatred, condemning it to hell, the bitter poison in your own heart will end up condemning you to hell. And that's not love either.

IN the end, psychotherapy is all about the adult part of the personality finally listening to the frightened child part tell its story—and taking adult responsibility for the healing process that the child part cannot manage on its own. For the psychotherapy, then, "Do you believe me?" is not a question about facts but a question about inner, emotional respect.

TO heal those old wounds of abuse, though, as an adult you must look back with sorrow—not guilt—on all of your failures to speak up as a child. Acknowledge the pain, and the sadness, and the fear—and the anger—of not having the protection and guidance your parents should have provided for you. Realize that, if they had provided proper guidance, you would have learned how to defend yourself appropriately. Then do all it takes, now, to learn to speak with honesty and integrity in the present.

YOU can begin this process psychologically by acknowledging your "human feelings or emotions"—all of them: the good, the bad, and the "ugly." See them for what they are in their full reality. Look clearly at the childhood wounds you have suffered from family dysfunction: the lies, the game-playing, the manipulation, the hypocrisy.

Then see your psychological defenses—the defenses that protect you from honestly acknowledging the truth of your emotional pain—for what they are, in their full reality. Open your eyes and stop hiding from yourself: stop defiling your own body, and stop using other persons as objects for your own narcissistic fulfillment.

Then detach yourself from all the self-indulgent satisfactions of the social world that, until now, have pushed God out of your life.

WHAT can you do, then? You cannot force yourself to love, but you can do whatever it takes to remove the obstacles to real love. Endeavor, through prayer and scrutiny, to look back into your past with honesty to feel the pain you have been denying, to identify the family behaviors that caused you to fear love, and to embrace and transform that fear.

This is hard work. It means that once you open up the door to your suppressed emotions you run the risk of letting your anger out as well. This, however, is really not as bad as it may seem. If you can learn to acknowledge and understand your angry impulses, rather than shut down any process that would reveal them to you, you can then learn to make a conscious effort to refuse to carry out those impulses. Instead of allowing your impulses to push you right into sin, you can let those angry impulses be warning signs that you have been emotionally hurt somehow, you can then turn back to examine that hurt honestly, and you can then turn to prayer for assistance. Pray for God to protect you, pray for the repentance of those who have hurt you, and pray for your ability to grow in love because of your trials—and pray especially that you can remain in a place of love regardless of what others do around you.

THE whole point of psychotherapy is to learn that there are very specific environmental triggers for your feelings. Recognize the triggers, first, and then recognize the emotional "bridge" that goes back to childhood wounds. Learn to look for the actual events (notice the plural) that have been bothering you recently. Take each one separately. What are all the feelings about that event? Frustration? Helplessness? Abandonment? Betrayal? Fear? (It won't be just anger, because anger is the final, hostile reaction to all the other feelings.)

When you have these emotions all separated out, then you have an idea of what is really happening to you, apart from the anger. Then you can deal with each event separately, according to the emotions specific to that event. It's your choice: do something constructive and creative about each problem individually, or, well, get angry about everything and stew in it.

WHEN you feel injured, it will be humanly natural to want to take matters into your own hands to get revenge. So pay attention to the fantasies of revenge that spring up in front of you, but resist the temptation to act on them. When someone hurts you, resist the temptation to respond with sarcasm or arguments or hostility or cursing. Look to divine justice, not to bitter revenge.

And when things, rather than other persons, obstruct you—such as traffic lights that turn red when you're in a hurry, or things that break when you're under pressure to get a job done—accept it quietly and obediently as God's wise intervention for your guidance.

Say, in prayer to God, "All right. This is teaching me something, and in due time I will understand. Right now I don't know why this is happening, but since this is what You want, then I will accept it. I trust in You in all things. But it hurts! So please give me the strength and courage to get me through this."

ONE key psychological experience in all this is the feeling that what happened to you isn't fair, and that other persons are escaping blame for your suffering. This is a valid feeling, for, indeed, all feelings are valid.

But spiritual healing requires you to take a step beyond finger pointing, blame, and revenge. It requires you to go beyond what is natural, or common, in the world of ordinary human behavior. It requires you to love others and pray for their repentance no matter what they do to you. For the whole point of spiritual healing is to purge your heart of ordinary self-focused human behavior—or sin—

and to live within God Himself, fully trusting in divine mercy.

So even though you may feel that what others do is not fair, as you bring that feeling into full consciousness it will be necessary to realize that in God there is nothing fair or unfair. It's all love. Under His guidance, everything works out for the greater good of all—if only we get out of the way by not dwelling in hatred and not insisting on our own ideas of revenge.

Up till now you have been stewing in it, and that's why everything seems so oppressive and foul underneath the surface of a nice social demeanor. If I'm wrong, then why are you in psychotherapy in the first place? Most likely, everything in your life is all caught up in a big snarl of childhood hurt.

So, if you go through this healing process, you will learn to free your hidden anger from its dark, silent prison. Having thus set it free, and having thus cleansed yourself of its stains, you will also be free of something else. You will be free of feeling like a victim and free of secretly blaming your parents, because as long as you keep your anger hidden, you remain emotionally disabled, and as long as you remain emotionally disabled, you are throwing your disability in your parents' faces to accuse them of their faults.

Once you acknowledge the core of your anger and stop unconsciously wishing harm on your parents, you can forgive your parents. Then you will be healed, and then you can turn to the whole world with real love in your heart.

13 HONESTY

EVERYTHING in psychology has a price. If you open your mouth to speak the truth, you pay a price. If you keep your mouth shut in fear, you pay a price. Psychology, therefore, teaches us that we cannot "opt out" of life. Even those who choose life-styles counter to the prevailing culture still live a cultural life-style. Even those who commit suicide do not reject culture; they very clearly make a cultural statement about their lack of hope and their unwillingness to face up to the truth of their unconscious past.

So if you want to make psychological changes in your life, you have to pay a price. No matter what anyone has ever done to you, you—and you alone—have to take personal responsibility for your healing. It will cost money, and time, and suffering. But the reward of liberty from cultural illusions is priceless.

WE are all liars and hypocrites, and we all make excuses for ourselves. In our legal and political systems, "truth" is nothing more than what we choose to believe in the moment. Our culture is all a fraud. But hardly anyone wants to admit it.

Now, if you call someone a liar, you will get one of two responses. If the person is wise, he or she will say, "Yes, I know." Being aware of the extent of his or her unconscious motivations, this person has the healing option of emptying the self of pride in order to find true honesty. But persons who are psychologically unaware and bristling with defenses will angrily blurt out, "How dare you! Take that back or else!" And the sad thing is that in defending themselves against the reality of their lies and hypocrisy, these persons become liars and hypocrites all the more.

THEREFORE, your lies become cunning weapons of revenge in a psychological battle to inflict pain on those who hurt you. That is, when someone treats you critically, you feel hurt, shamed, and afraid; and then, as an angry response to that hurt, you will tell lies in a fabricated sense of invulnerability to hide your painful shame while causing injury to that person.

The only solution to all these lies is to face up to the emotional pain of feeling misunderstood and inadequate. Track that pain back to its origins in childhood and see it honestly for what it was. Understand just how you were ignored or neglected. Understand how much you feared—and still fear—"not knowing" and being abandoned. Understand how you can blame yourself for not knowing. Understand the anger simmering in your unconscious. Understand how you can hurt yourself in the process of giving others what they "deserve."

YOU cannot have meaningful and honest interactions

with others if you persist in clinging, deep in your heart, to psychological defense mechanisms that shield you from that very pain. How can you be genuine with another person if you're always protecting yourself with your own wits? In the past, particularly as a child, blame, resentment, and anger may have served to ensure your survival by masking your hurt and vulnerability, but in reality these things are totally opposed to integrity and real love.

AND that is the problem with honesty. When you grow up in a dysfunctional family accustomed to lies and deceit, it can feel as if you are doing something wrong if you start telling the truth. When you are so used to fraud, the truth not only seems false, it seems dangerous.

CO-DEPENDENT behavior is a matter of someone enabling (e.g., making excuses for, or lying for) someone whose social life is crumbling because of an addiction. The sad truth is that whenever you have "too much to lose" to be honest about the addict's behavior, then you are essentially as dependent on the addiction as the addict.

REMEMBER: it was unnamed dishonesty—perhaps in your own family—that made you suicidal or self-destructive in the first place. Many children who have been wounded by this dishonesty often reach a point in their lives at which they resolve that they will never allow themselves to be deceived by anyone ever again. And then, sadly, for the rest of their lives they are deceived by their own pride.

HONESTY involves learning how to express openly to another person the fullness of your immediate inner experience, by setting aside all your characteristic psychological defenses. To do that, you have to come to terms with the emotional pain that caused those defenses to come into being in the first place. That pain originated through parental and other social interactions in your childhood, but, just as you continue to encounter these same sorts of painful feelings through social interactions in your adult life, you will also encounter these feelings as a result of interactions between you and your psychotherapist. This is the essence of the therapeutic relationship. You confront your pain directly in psychotherapy, without running from it, so that you can heal it and transform it.

EMOTIONAL awareness, therefore, is a psychological tool that provides protection from sin. Interpersonal conflicts result from failed emotional communication. Temptations do not just appear out of nowhere; behind every temptation is an emotional reaction to some event that has shaken your self-confidence. It is impossible to stay in the place of purity of heart if you fail to understand your emotional reactions to the events around you.

Thus through psychotherapy you can learn to respond to every moment of the present with a complete understanding of the emotions involved—and this understanding gives you the ability to respond honestly and appropriately to the situation.

For example, if someone says something that hurts you, you can say to yourself, "OK. I'm feeling helpless and abandoned." In the midst of these feelings, you can recognize how you responded defensively to similar feelings as a child. Then you can choose an appropriate, non-defensive, mature, and psychologically honest response to your current feelings.

But if you haven't done your psychological work, instead of naming your feelings you will just feel a vague yucky inadequacy and then get angry or go off and drown the yuck with food or drugs or some other dysfunctional behavior. The sad thing is that when you drown the yuck, right along with it you drown the possibility of healing.

NOT all psychological defenses are unhealthy, however; many defenses, such as humor, serve a highly functional purpose. Thus we really cannot "escape" our defenses because we are humans of the flesh. With genuine trust in God, however, we can be set free from our defensive—and often unconscious—tendency to hide our pain from ourselves. And once we stop hiding our pain from ourselves we can stop hiding our pain from God, and then we can live honest religious lifestyles.

TO act with kindness in spite of what you are feeling does not mean that you are being dishonest. If you act with kindness in spite of the fact that you would like to take pleasure in vengeance, you are acting with love because God calls us to act with love, and to follow His commands means that you are being honest about your faith.

SO, yes, the truth can taste strange, and it can be terrifying—but when you encounter it honestly and without psychological weapons you will discover a courage you can never learn through trying to defeat your enemies.

REFLECT on why God gave us *free will*. If we couldn't say "No" to God, our saying "Yes" to God would be meaningless. In a similar way, if we cannot acknowledge our capacity to hurt others—indeed, our *desire* to hurt others—when they hurt us, then we cannot express our love for them through a refusal to hurt them. Without an honesty about our hatred for others, any good we do for them is just an act of duty; it's not really an act of love. To love others is to wish them good, especially by refusing to do them the harm that, somewhere in the recesses of our minds, we would like to do to them.

Consequently, to love others you must first know that you want to hurt them; then, as an act of love, you can refuse to carry out that hurtful impulse.

MANY persons balk at the idea of emotional honesty for fear of its social consequences. "But if I'm honest with others, they will reject me and I will lose their love," you might say. Well, there is really only one answer to this concern: *If others reject you because you are honest, then you never had their love in the first place.* All you risk losing by being honest is the illusion of someone's love. In this sense, you really have nothing to lose in being honest because you have already lost it anyway.

THOSE who have the most to gain have the greatest desire to deceive. Those who have the least to gain—and who want nothing, and who give everything in complete honesty—can love perfectly. And this perfect, real love is no illusion.

14 HOPE

WE watch television and sports and we read newspa-
pers and magazines in the *hope of seeing something* that will
make us feel good about ourselves. We play sports and
video games in the *hope of accomplishing something* that will
make us feel good about ourselves. We listen to music and
chat on cell phones in the *hope of hearing something* that
will make us feel good about ourselves. We make food
into an addiction in the *hope of smelling and tasting something* that will make us feel good about ourselves. And we
make sexuality into the most pervasively sought-after entertainment of all, in the *hope of seeing, hearing, smelling,
tasting, and accomplishing something* that will make us feel
good about ourselves.

But be careful here not to deceive yourself by attribut-
ing any deep meaning to these "hopes." Don't believe for
a moment that there is such a thing as "wholesome entertainment." The desire to be entertained—to be soothed,
satisfied, and fulfilled—is, at its core, a social "religion"
unto itself that serves the god of narcissistic happiness in
the frenzied quest to feel good about our bodies while ig-
noring the most poignant hopes of our lost souls.

WITH all of our knowledge hanging like a deceptive veil over the agony of being, we stand helplessly under the psychological law of lack and limitation. Trapped in this wretched state, therefore, we have only one hope: to understand the soul.

PSYCHOLOGY can teach us not only that our social world is a "fraud" but also that it is possible to recognize and heal the pain we felt as children when we experienced the world's fraud. Psychology can teach us to speak about those childhood wounds rather than keep them as dark secrets hidden away within ourselves, wrapped in feelings of victimization. Psychology can teach us to let go of bitterness and hatred and to show compassion and love for those secrets, in the hope of healing them, rather than killing them. But if those secrets are not healed they become our unconscious enemies—and we become terrorists in a battle against our own pain.

PSYCHOLOGICAL trauma, especially childhood sexual abuse, can leave you with a confused mass of ordinary human emotions. But this confusion can feel so painful that your primary psychological defense to save your life will be to "get away" from it all and to turn your back on divine values such as love and forgiveness, and mercy. It's a sad thing for this to happen, even though it may be the only way for the child to survive.

Thus you will find yourself in a living hell with recourse to nothing but empty human weapons of anger, bitterness, and fear. And the guilt will linger as an unconscious secret that you will struggle to hide—and run from—for the rest of your life.

If, through the process of spiritual purgation, you have the courage to face all those emotions related to the abuse, tease them apart, and understand how each one affects your behavior, then there is real hope. Otherwise you will spend the rest of your life reacting automatically and blindly to your emotions, blaming others and feeling victimized by circumstances that are really of your own making.

IT can happen that persons who teach the principles of real peace will be persecuted by those who have too much to lose by listening to the truth. To die, if necessary, under such persecution is martyrdom. Martyrs proclaim their refusal to hate, for in blessing even those who persecute them they keep open the hope that the persecutors may repent their mistakes. And this explains why no one who is killed for his or her political opposition to rivals, who is killed in the act of killing others, or who commits suicide—by itself or in the course of killing others—can be a martyr, for all these acts psychologically foreclose all hope of forgiveness and healing.

IF your expectations are positive, you will make your best effort, and you will likely succeed. But if your expectations are negative you will almost certainly fail.

Consider a child who out of curiosity tries to do something he has never done before; for example, say the child has just seen a golfer and now tries to hit a stone with a stick. His concerned parent yells at him, "You can't do that!" Wouldn't it be nicer if the parent had said, "I'm not sure it will work that way. It may or it may not. Let's try, and if it doesn't work, we'll find out why." Which parental reaction do you think will encourage the child to become creative and successful?

Unfortunately, the same sort of negative parental criticism is unwittingly given out by many physicians time and time again. It's common for a physician, face grim with an air of authority and finality, to say, "I'm sorry. There's nothing that can be done." How many people lose all hope then and there, right in the supposed office of healing, when they have expectancies of failure planted in them by their own physicians?

NOTE carefully that in trying to overcome an addiction you will immediately encounter a frustrating paradox: *thinking about the negative consequences of an addiction will only increase the desire for the addictive substance.* So why does this happen? Well, the psychological defense at the core of any addiction is denial, so when contemplating any negative idea (such as getting cancer from smoking), your mind will crave the intense pleasure of the addiction as a way to override (i.e., deny) the frightening idea.

Therefore, even though it is important to know the negative consequences of the addiction, the fear of those consequences in itself won't be nearly so much a motivation for overcoming the addiction as will be the hope of positive changes. Consequently, those positive changes need to be visualized very, very clearly.

IN spite of our inclinations to self-love and self-will, in spite of our knowing that we can never do enough, in spite of all we don't know, in spite of all our fear of making mistakes, in spite of all the wretchedness that separates us from God, we still have one chain of hope.

- We can *admit* that apart from God we truly are wretched {period}.

- In admitting it, we can *face* the helplessness and pain of it without hiding it in the unconscious through denial.

- In facing it, we can *see* that even if we avoid all major sin we still sin constantly in small ways.

- In seeing all those small sins through the illumination of grace we will be *moved* to love God more deeply, to repent those sins, to learn from them, and to seek greater and greater purification from our wretchedness.

And here, at the end of the chain, we find ourselves being wretched {gracefully} in God's love. The more we admit our wretchedness, and the more we are willing to learn from our mistakes, the more we gain access to divine grace.

So ultimately we discover a great irony. When we stop trying to use psychological defenses to hide our being wretched {period}, and when we die to ourselves by detaching ourselves from the world's attachment to sin, and when we give up trying to make ourselves feel good through our own efforts with our own bodies, then—in our very own self-examination—we find the opening to divine grace.

We can then be wretched {gracefully}, freed from that trap of hopelessness that is sealed and locked, like the last sentence of a paragraph, with the wretched period of sin.

IF you want to live a holy life, keep your heart focused on your destination. It doesn't matter if you're not there yet. It doesn't matter how far you have to go. Just keep your heart focused on God, and let hope guide your progress.

RESOLVE to become a "father" to yourself. Instead of staying stuck in blaming your father for what you don't have, and in unconsciously punishing him with your failures, focus on taking personal responsibility to provide for yourself with what has until now been lacking in you. This is easier said than done, so there are three things you can hope in to overcome your despair.

- Hope in psychological guidance, such as you are now receiving from me and my writing, and do whatever it takes to learn from it.

- Hope also in a growing cooperation with your own unconscious, so that your unconscious will be an ally in learning. Realize that your

unconscious is not "out to get you"; it is, in essence, the truth of your life, which, until now,
you have largely suppressed because, in not
having your father's guidance in how to appre-
ciate it, you have feared it. Through your psychological work of healing you will find that
your unconscious can be a trusted source of
enlightenment.

- Hope also in prayer, which will become more
  and more meaningful to you as you let go of
  your anger at your father and come to see God
  not as a reflection of your father's failures but
  as He really is: your truest and deepest hope.

15   HUMILITY

To live in humility is to live always in total confidence of God's love, protection, and guidance and therefore to have no concern for yourself when others insult you—or praise you.

Humility, therefore, is actually a sign of great courage and deep spiritual understanding. In humility there is no fear. In humility there is no timidity. In humility there is only confidence—confidence, not in the self, but in God's loving protection.

Consider the nature of water, a weak and lowly substance that flows freely around all obstacles. If you live a life of the same "humility" as water, even the jaws of hell cannot bite into you. But the more solid you become in the pride of your own strength to avenge yourself against insult, the more those jaws have to grasp onto—and once they have you, you can't fight free, no matter how many bandoliers you have draped over your shoulders.

So, in the end, all fantasy literature must encounter its

own moral failure. It's just not possible to use glamour and power to convey the deep meaning of spiritual humility and self-surrender. And, to be perfectly blunt, a devout life grounded in quiet faith and the patient endurance of adversity is, by entertainment standards, simply boring.

EVEN though a life of humility depends on emotional honesty, the psychological task of attaining humility is not about "feeling emotions fully" but in (a) feeling all the emotions connected to a particular event; (b) recognizing the thoughts associated with any particular emotion; and (c) discovering the crippling effects those thoughts have had on your life.

In working through this process, you will come to understand how various events of your life have led you to develop various unconscious psychological defense mechanisms; furthermore, you will learn that various talents and hopes within you have gone unfulfilled and that now, in true humility, you can make serious changes to your life by developing new behaviors.

THREE aspects of humility: a) to set aside your attempts to make yourself feel "special" through the acceptance and admiration of others; (b) to overcome your repugnance to feeling emotionally hurt by others; and (c) to seek the good of others in all things, setting aside all competition, even at your own expense.

Still, let's be careful that this is done in a psychologically healthy manner.

First, it's good when our work is recognized and appreciated; the spiritual point is that we shouldn't crave this admiration as an aspect of a personal identity, but that we endeavor to accept all benefits of our work in praise of God, and in whose service we do our work.

Second, we all feel hurt when someone insults us; still, the spiritual point is that we don't need to build up psychological defenses to protect ourselves from the pain of being insulted if only, even in our deepest hurt, we always endeavor to trust in God, Who alone will protect us from all danger.

Finally, although "placing others first" runs counter to natural self-preservation, the spiritual point is that, if we really trust in God, not only can we stop competing with others to satisfy our pride but also we can endeavor to notice the needs of others, looking on others with compassion, in the hope that they might be saved from destruction because of their own desperate obsession with self-preservation. Nevertheless, our concern for others must not take on a form of masochism or self-defilement; in all of our charity to others we must never relinquish the responsibility of developing our talents to the fullest, so that we can serve God effectively and joyfully, in pure love.

IF any discrepancy does arise between *detachment from the world* and *love*, it's the result of pride. Pride is simply the narcissistic desire to stand apart from others so that you can think of yourself as being "special." As you mention, pride can trick us into believing we are doing God's will when really we are serving our own self-interests.

You can best protect yourself from the sin of pride by

cultivating the opposite virtue: humility. Think of humility, in its essence, as such a complete awareness of the awesome mystery of God's love that you have no other desire than to be detached from all that is not holy and to pray constantly for the conversion of all that is not holy.

Pride, we can note, seeks only its own glory. Pride may accept the idea of serving God, intellectually, but it rejects the personal suffering of carrying that service deep into the heart. Therefore, pride does not know how to pray for others, and, though it might cause you to speak words of prayer, your heart will remain cold, hard, and aloof.

YOU can see visions, hear locutions, and pray in tongues, but what good are these things if they do not lead you into ever deeper humility and ever greater acts of suffering and self-sacrifice for the sake of mercy to others?

KNOWING—that is, anticipating—what might happen next is a characteristic defensive desire of children in dysfunctional families. After all, if they can guess an irrational parent's next move, they might be able to avoid an ugly family scene.

To such children, then, it's a loathsome thing to admit, "I don't know."

This explains why, if you offer some piece of information to a person who grew up in a dysfunctional family, his or her response will likely not be a humble "Thank you" but will be a quickly retorted "I know!"

WHAT, then should you do? Well, you need to learn

humility. You need to shatter the illusions of common "love" and discover real love: the ability to seek the good of another without regard for personal satisfaction or gain. Moreover, this real love does not depend on being smart; it's simply a humble, honest human interaction.

So stop fighting the world with your intellect because of what you're not getting from the world, and, instead of rage, give to the world what you have never received: real love. And, because you will likely never find a psychotherapist smarter than you are, go back to your current psychotherapist and teach her real love by your willingness to allow her to teach you humble, illusion-free trust and honesty.

IN intense psychotherapy with someone who really knows his job you will learn wisdom and humility as you encounter them in the healing process. But until you reach that place of full emotional commitment to looking beyond what you merely *think* so as to peer deep into your unconscious motivation, you will always be trying to argue with life (and with your psychotherapist) the same way adults argue with a child. It will seem that life, in all its empty vanity, is treating you just like a distracted parent treats a child: with expectations, not nurturing. You will want desperately to rise above everything that seems foolish and to poke holes in it with brilliant intellect.

"POSTPARTUM depression" need not be a clinical depression, and it need not even be associated with childbirth. In fact, many events in life, when successfully completed, can bring on a sense of temporary "depression."

I myself felt sick and depressed when I successfully passed all my comprehensive exams on the way to my Ph.D. degree. The same thing happened when I passed my licensing exams for my psychologist license, and, on the very afternoon that I passed my flight exam for my private pilot's license, I developed flu symptoms that lasted for two days of misery.

All of this really derives from the existential experience of investing tremendous energy to achieve something special—and then, when it is finally achieved, feeling a profound inner void. I now understand that this is a spiritual problem, for when we fail to live with devout humility and emptiness of self—as I sadly failed to do in those years—we are blind to any grounding in spiritual stability, and we instead skip from one social accomplishment to another, with gaps of despair in between.

THOSE who find their "knowing" in the social world are too arrogant and self-sufficient to look beyond humanism, and for that very reason they are always being deceived. But for those who aren't deceived, God—the epitome of what's hidden from human eyes—resides beyond the veil of human knowledge. In fact, to push past one's weakness and admit frankly that there is something more beyond "knowing" is a confession in its own right: a confession that we aren't deceived by the veil, a confession that what we are looking for is profound humility before God, and a confession that, without God, we are broken and wretched creatures, no matter how much we know, or think we know, about the world.

16 IDENTITY

FROM all the things that appeal to us in the world, we create images of how we want to see ourselves, and then we set about making ourselves "seen" in the world so our images can be reflected back to us through the desire of others. Whether it's business suits or purple hair and pierced lips, an image is an image. Some persons desire to be desired with such desperate intensity that you can actually see in their eyes the inner emptiness they seek to fill.

YOU might go to great expense to project an image into the world. You might explain yourself in endless detail to others so they will get the "true" picture of you. You might offer your identity to the world as if it were a bowl of jewels. But you're offering only a plate of stones.

AS long as you derive your identity from the world around you, you have to be concerned about losing it. Like a dragon sitting greedily on its hoard of treasure, your entire being will be caught up in defending what you are most afraid to lose.

As infants, we are just a jumble of diverse biological processes over which we have no authority, and our first task in life is to develop a coherent identity which "pulls together" this fragmented confusion. This identity may give the appearance of a unified personality, but it really is just a psychological illusion that hides our essential human vulnerability and weakness. And so, when anything or anyone threatens us with the truth of our essential fragmentation, the quickest, easiest, and most common defense available—to hide the truth of our weakness and to give the illusion that we possess some sort of power—is aggression.

Remember—an event is traumatic because it disrupts your previously secure sense of self. Consider that wild animals live with a sharp awareness of perpetual danger, yet most people live with a naive—and deceptive—sense of safety and security to the point of denying their basic vulnerability and fragmented sense of self. So when something disastrous happens, the psychological damage from the shattering of one's illusions about life and identity may be more problematic than any physical damage.

In fact, all the "pieces of the world" that we use as identifications to construct our own identities are, in the end, nothing but illusions. That's why Posttraumatic Stress Disorder (PTSD) is nothing but the shocking and painful awareness of what we already know but prefer to hide. The trauma that has brought us just inches from death shows us with shocking clarity that all our defenses against death are just empty illusions.

UNDERSTAND, then, that you are vulnerable to being manipulated by the "desire of the Other" in so far as you seek your identity—that is, your feeling of social acceptance—in other persons around you. As long as you crave the feeling of approval and belonging so as to feel good about yourself, you will be susceptible to desiring whatever the Other shows you as an image of approval and belonging. And that image can be anything: a physical object, physical or emotional pleasure, an ideology, or even "spirituality" itself.

NO, your children don't see living faith. Your children don't see protection from evil. Your children don't see genuine, fruitful devotion. Instead, they see your external acts of devotion as meaningless because they see all the other things you do, or your husband or wife does, that contradict the living faith. And so you lose credibility. And when the parents lose credibility, the children feel abandoned, and, in frustration and fear, they turn to the illusions of the social world around them for identity and acceptance.

RIGHT now, with all your illusions wrapped around you, you are dwelling in spiritual blindness, even though you deny it. Of course you can't see it. Who could?

THE best way to develop psychological insight is to turn away from social "outsight"—that is, attachment to social identifications that merely cover over our inner confusion and turmoil with a surface feeling of acceptance by others. So, considering that unconscious psychological conflicts more often than not lead us away from complete trust in God and right into spiritual disobedience, it would be prudent to err on the side of too much detachment from social "outsight" than too little.

DO anything you can to disentangle yourself from the social illusions of the *ego*. Personality disorders have their essential basis in defending ego "identity" and protecting it from interpersonal threat, so you will benefit much to learn, as the psychoanalyst Jacques Lacan taught, that "I" is an illusion. Instead of filling yourself with repetitive assertions of what "I want" and what "I need" and what "I deserve" and what "I fear," turn your attention to what you can give to others—that is, to all the emotionally wounded individuals in this world—through personal sacrifice and prayer. This, after all, is what real love is all about, whereas personality disorders, in one way or another, do their psychological best to maintain your fear of love.

MAYBE you will say, "Wait a minute. What can I give? I feel like mush inside. I'm already empty. I feel barren. It feels as if I have no identity. I have nothing to give." Well, there is always something to give up, something that everyone holds on to as a final defense: you can give up the pride of being a victim, along with its hope to taste revenge for all the hurt and abuse you have ever suffered.

REAL love, therefore, forsakes the prestige offered by

the culture in its illusions. And, when we have been taught from childhood to covet this prestige as our very identity, is it any wonder that we fear love?

Far easier—and safer—isn't it, to hide behind illusions and games of wealth, power, violence, intrigue, and seduction?

SO the more you let go of your "identity"—the more you die to yourself in perfect humility—the less you have to defend; and the less you have to defend, the less reason you have for anger.

IN fact, it's our desperate need to find a sense of "self" through identification with the social world that keeps us enslaved to the fear that the fraud of our "selves" will be discovered. Only when we die to ourselves in God do we experience the peace and security of His real presence that can never be lost.

17 LOVE

THE common, or popular, view of love involves an element of receiving something. "I love chocolate" really means that "I enjoy getting the experience of the taste of chocolate." Similarly, "I love you" commonly implies "I enjoy touching your body" or "I enjoy believing that you will give me security or protection" or "I enjoy having sex with you" or "I want to have sex with you".

AS shocking as it might sound, most of us who claim to be "loving" are not giving selflessly. Instead, we are addressing a covert psychological desire to avoid being abandoned. Sad to say, the apparent generosity of common "love" is more an act of bribery than of real love.

TO most persons today "love" means satisfaction. It means happiness. It means having one's emotional emptiness filled with, well . . . just about anything, as long as it's filling. It means "I'm OK, you're OK." In all its meanings, "love" means self-indulgence.

But in this definition of "love" cleverly constructed to suit popular culture, something is missing: sin. In a popular culture of narcissism in which anything that serves the "self" is acceptable, *sin*—the narcissistic preoccupation with immediate desires that leaves little, if any, altruistic awareness of anyone or anything else in the environment—is robbed of its definition And that's precisely where everything goes wrong; when anything is socially permissible, real love is trumped and defiled by common "love."

YOU could program your computer to say, "I love you" every morning when you turn it on, but that synthesized message wouldn't be love, would it? A computer simply does what it is told to do, and, philosophically, if you cannot say "No" your saying "Yes" is meaningless.

Therefore, love must be a free choice—an act of free will.

Consequently, many things that we commonly call "love" are not love at all. Infatuation. Obsession. Fatal attraction. Lust. We call them love but they have nothing to do with real love because they enslave us to illusions.

IT'S impossible to heal your own emotional brokenness through the body of another person as mortal and broken as you are.

This truth can be approximated by the question, "What is the sound of one hand clapping?"

For example, I have seen both men and women who have tried to seduce a woman to get from her the nurturing and attention they never received from their mothers. And I have seen both women and men who have tried to seduce a man to get from him the protection and attention they never received from their fathers. And in the end it's all an impossibility. The moral is simple, and cuts across the board, male and female, heterosexual and homosexual: you can never seduce your despair, and you can never find real love through any form of sexual activity.

Thus, one does not need a "sex life" to be a good person. Notice, though, that a good person is not the same as a good citizen. A good citizen is an insatiable consumer, and, because of the efforts of Madison Avenue and Hollywood, eroticism has become a prime consumer activity. So let's give a round of applause to Madison Avenue and Hollywood. Ah, can you hear it—the pathetic sound of one hand clapping?

IN its proper place, peer pressure does have a value because it can help you avoid certain behaviors. For example, in regard to overcoming addictions, peer pressure can be helpful in supporting you to avoid the use of alcohol, drugs, cigarettes, and angry violence.

But peer pressure cannot make you acquire virtue. Virtue is an expression of love, and love is an act of free will, and so, if you are pressured into doing something, especially if the pressure causes you to violate your personal boundaries, it is not an act of love.

Keep in mind, therefore, that genuine religion is a matter of pure love which spreads through a quiet, humble demonstration of self-sacrifice despite tribulations and persecution. Consequently, if you do anything to gain the acceptance of others, or to keep them from rejecting you, it's a defilement of love, and, in the spiritual sense, it's all a fraud.

WE love God because He created us to share in His love. God *is* love. He is not some deluded emperor who demands adoration from everyone around him to satisfy his inflated ego. Souls who love God don't serve Him because He demands their obedience like an irrational parent; souls who love God love Him *in* love *for the sake of* love, and, through His grace, they *become* love.

I have seen it over and over again: people are all smiles and devotional behavior on the surface, but once they are pushed the slightest bit against their own will they become very hostile, very quickly. For most people, love is just an intellectual concept—a surface scratch. So understand that love doesn't get real until, as an expression of sacrifice, obedience, and prayer, it rips right into the depths of your heart.

REAL love is far more difficult than common "love" because real love is given, not received—and certainly not made—and it must be given with no expectation or hope of getting anything in return.

LOVE is an act of will, not something that you "fall" into. You can fall into desperate desire, and you can fall into fatal attraction, but you can't fall into love.

IN the end, then, you didn't really fall in love with him,

you became enamored of the hope that you might, through your own efforts, overcome his anger at you. This isn't being uplifted to the level of love, it's being reduced to the level of your own childhood trauma.

THIS all goes to show that it's easy enough to "love" those who "love" us: parents who protect us, "partners" who make us feel received, animals who never threaten us. But can we love those who annoy us . . . irritate us . . . obstruct us . . . scorn us . . . hate us? Can we love our enemies? That's the real test of *real* love.

YOU say you want to be loved? Well, keep in mind that if you curse others, there will come a time when you will be cursed. If you hate others, there will come a time when you will be hated. And if you love others, well, there will come a time when you will be loved.

UNDERSTAND that genuine religion is not a matter of knowledge for its own sake. It is not a matter of intellectual prowess or of philosophy. It is not a matter of arguing with others. It is not a matter of displaying your holiness for others to see and admire. It is not a matter of visions and ecstasies. It is simply a matter of emptiness of self and pure love.

IN one moment, they hear about horrific tortures inflicted on the martyrs—beatings, stabbings, bodies torn apart and burned. They pray to find strength from the martyrs' courage and to rejoice in the martyrs' triumph. Then, no sooner have they turned around than they experience a tiny pinprick of an insult or inconvenience, and they fly into a rage. What happened to the prayers that were on their lips just moments ago? Where have all the martyrs gone? Where has *love* gone?

WHAT is fasting all about anyway? Isn't it about realizing that you need to hunger for God as much as you hunger for food? To put a piece of grass in your mouth during a fast, you're "soothing" yourself—however unconsciously—and that detracts from your hunger for God. So the grass really does break the fast. The answer doesn't depend on nitpicking about how insignificant the grass may be, or how minuscule are the nutrients in it. It has nothing to do with a legal approach that looks for loopholes, because if you look for loopholes in love, it's not love in the first place. And in that you have the essence of real love: no loopholes, just pure love.

THIS leads, then, to the understanding of why we praise God. Praise is the only way for the created to love the creator. When we praise God, therefore, we enter into love for Him. We praise God not because He needs praise to soothe feelings of insecurity; nor do we praise Him because He is a narcissist who feeds on admiration. We praise Him because, in praising Him, we become love. God does not need our praise, but, for our own "sanity," we need our praises of Him.

IT was out of a true understanding of the difference between common "love" and real love that a man such as Saint Francis of Assisi was led—led right to the point, actually—to pray that he might seek "not so much to be loved as to love."

REAL love, therefore, is not about getting noticed or feeling accepted. Real love is a process of *giving*—not the giving of material things that merely bribe others to like us, but the giving of qualities such as patience, kindness, compassion, understanding, mercy, forbearance, and forgiveness, qualities whose ultimate purpose is the good of other souls.

AS long as you are concerned about what you can get from life, you will always be dissatisfied. Everything material—food, entertainment, drugs, erotic pleasure—passes quickly only to leave us overpowered by cravings for more. Real love, however, endures every insult peacefully and so it can never be overpowered by anything.

BUT consider this more deeply. What does all of this mean, psychologically? Taking what you want . . . making yourself seen . . . having power . . . feeling desired . . . feeling protected? Isn't this all a compensation for feelings of inferiority, weakness, and vulnerability? It's all an immediate way of getting something to overcome the emotional hurt of childhood insecurity. Romance, therefore, is a game, a way to even the score with the emotional pains of childhood.

Real love, in contrast, is not a game—it's reality raised

to the level of the divine.

LOVE, after all, never misses the point, and so it never needs to prove anything.

NOW, many persons today claim to love God. But do they *really* love Him? Are they willing to do *anything* it takes to purify themselves for His service? Are they willing to love their enemies—that is, to endure peacefully the suffering caused by their enemies and to offer it as a prayerful sacrifice for the repentance and conversion of those very enemies? Or, instead of really loving God, do they simply take satisfaction in the *idea* of loving Him and let real love wither and die in the darkness of their hearts?

THEREFORE, without loving God it's impossible to love ourselves with anything more than narcissism or our neighbors with anything more than lust.

THE problem is that, because of the way your parents treated you, you fear love—and, because you fear love, you have been suppressing your anger just enough to keep it out of sight but not enough to prevent it from leaking out when you are most vulnerable. In your case, you are most vulnerable when others' lack of respect for your sense of duty causes you to catch a momentary glimpse of the truth that duty is not love. Your anger is just a puff of smoke—a magician's trick—that allows you to quickly remove from sight your lack of love for God and replace it with your indignation that others lack love for God.

STILL, deep in your soul, you do want God's love, just as you crave the love of the father who angers you. You will never see this love, however, by denying your anger. Anger—even unconscious anger—makes love impossible. But if only you acknowledge the anger, understand it, and heal the hurt that lies beneath it, then you can forgive your father—and then you will be capable of real love.

KEEP in mind this analogy: fire does not burn itself—only that which is not fire is burned by fire. Thus, in the spiritual realm, God's love burns and torments whatever is not love. God's love burns and torments unrepentant souls who are "not love" because in this life they have chosen lifestyles defiant of love, thereby refusing the opportunity to become love.

GOD loves everyone, and He calls everyone into His love. But to accept this call we must give up everything that is not love.

GOD does not want us merely to know that He exists; God wants us to know *Him*. God wants us to know Him *as love*, and, by knowing love, to become love, and, in becoming love, to serve love, and, in serving love, to assist others in finding their way out of superficiality and into His real presence.

TO love God with all your heart and mind and soul, to

turn away from your sins and desire nothing but holy service to God, and to pray constantly that God's will be done in you, in your neighbor, and in the whole world: that is the soul's expression of love.

IT'S relatively easy to be simple and gentle—even nice—because simpleness and gentleness are often learned in childhood as psychological defenses to cope with the instability and conflict of a dysfunctional family. But unless you have a certain shrewdness about the world, you can easily be seduced into doing things that seem simple yet are really sinful and evil. Only when simpleness is more than a defense and derives from a deep love of God, and when you have a shrewdness that derives from a desire to not do anything that defiles love, can you truly respect yourself and be truly loving.

As long as you cling to the self-created belief that you are unlovable (as a psychological defense against admitting that your parents failed you in love) you won't be able to tolerate real love. You will crave it, and yet, at the same time, you will push it away in the belief that you are unworthy of it. Then, believing yourself unworthy of the real thing, you will unconsciously seek out imitations of love. Separated from real love, you will seek out "relationships," even if the relationship is with nothing more than a bottle of alcohol, your own body, or the fantasy of another person's acceptance of you.

Now, you say that you want "to love myself enough

to stop the feelings that I keep stuffing down in order to NOT hurt others." Well, this means that right now you are pushing your feelings out of awareness—that is, "stuffing" them—to avoid hurting others, and you think that it would be better to have no feelings at all—that is, to "stop" your feelings.

If you really were to love yourself, however, you would be able to love your feelings, and "to love your feelings" means that you could understand them rather than just get rid of them.

The real way to not hurt others is to learn to love yourself; to do this, then, endeavor to follow a step-by-step psychological process of emotional honesty. First, acknowledge exactly how you were hurt. Then admit to yourself your feelings of hurt. Then recognize your "natural" impulses of revenge that result from feeling hurt. Then make the decision not to act on those impulses, but, despite what you're feeling, to give to others your patience, kindness, compassion, forbearance, mercy, and forgiveness.

Follow this process and you will do good to yourself and to others. That's real love.

To love yourself, therefore, means overcoming two self-defeating tendencies.

On the one hand, loving yourself requires that you stop condemning yourself psychologically—to stop believing that God wants to condemn you. You may feel like garbage because of the way you were treated in childhood, but in God's eyes you are not garbage. In love, God created you at your conception, and in love He calls you to

Him always. To accept His calling, all you have to do is place yourself in obedience to God, treating your body with respect and treating your soul with ardent concern for its growth in purity by avoiding the defilement of inner evils.

On the other hand, loving yourself requires that you stop blaming yourself for your past failures. No matter how often and in what way you have fallen into those inner evils—no matter how wretched you feel—all is not lost if only you learn from your past mistakes and trust in God's infinite mercy.

AND you? Well, you fear love, and you can push love away, but you can't kill it.

YOU have within your heart the desire to love, but it has somehow been buried under fear because of what was lacking in your own childhood. When you were a child, abstract and dull rules were imposed on you, and you were left feeling empty and lazy. You did not experience religion as a matter of real love. Now, by the grace of God, you have the opportunity to embrace your faith and rediscover the love that God gave you in the beginning but that languished because it wasn't watered properly.

18 MERCY

IN its psychological sense, mercy means to withhold some—or all—of the punishment demanded by justice, if the guilty person shows deep sorrow for his or her behavior.

In its additional theological implications, mercy can also involve showing kindness to others in the hope that they might overcome their fear and, feeling sorrow for their sins, turn to God's mercy.

PSYCHOLOGICAL *fear* refers to a narcissistic concern about possible damage to our pride and safety. In contrast, *fear of God* refers to our humble awe and service before God's great glory and mercy. Thus, whereas psychological fear pulls us away from God, fear of God leads us directly into the embrace of divine love.

GOD is always offering His mercy, despite our arrogance. All we have to do is accept His mercy, despite our fears.

SOME psychological disorders have their own peculiar way of seeking protection from guilt with their own means, rather than by turning back to God and seeking His mercy.

- Individuals with *Obsessive-Compulsive Disorder* (OCD) hold the belief that guilt must be neutralized with ritualistic behaviors. Thus they trust in their own hands rather than turn to God's mercy.

- Individuals with *paranoia* suppress the awareness of their own guilt by projecting it onto the environment, thereby creating the belief that others are out to get them. Thus they trust in their own delusions rather than turn to God's mercy.

- Individuals with *depression* identify with their guilt, thus getting stuck in the self-condemning belief that they are "bad" and therefore deserve only misery. Thus they trust in their own punishment rather than turn to God's mercy.

SELF-CONDEMNATION and self-punishment usurp God's wisdom, and, in doing that, they push away God's mercy. As long as you're punishing yourself, you simply are denying any mercy that God could have for you.

That's why self-punishment is such a mistake: it's a sin in itself. Moreover, the irony is that if you presume to punish yourself for *your mistakes of self-punishment,* you stay locked in self-punishment and sin—forever.

THE problem, then, is that in our proud, hardened hearts we refuse to accept the mercy so graciously offered to us. In trying to defend our self-esteem from the emotional wounds of family dysfunction, we try to convince ourselves that we are self-sufficient, and we end up believing that begging for mercy is just another game—like all family games—that will lead to more humiliation.

MERCY—and love—are not just a matter of all-inclusive acceptance. It's not just a psychological matter of saying, "I'm OK, you're OK." Yes, God loves us, but our sins separate us from Him. Real love, therefore, calls us away from sin and into repentance. Real love doesn't just say, "Come, and join us." It also calls people to repent their sins. Real love calls people to you so you can inspire them to change their behavior.

DO not become angry at the sins of others, but think of the mercy that awaits them, if only they would repent their sins and accept God's mercy. And then pray and make sacrifices that they do accept it.

THUS you, being an instrument of God, have to show people that the things they "love" are, first of all, just illusions that hide their unconscious resentment and anger at God. In addition, all these illusions are just a way to deny God's mercy to others. Because if you fail to tell others that they are living in sin they can't repent, can they? If you fail in this, they will be destroyed—and you, through your obstinate disobedience, will die a slow spiritual suicide and will be destroyed as well.

To deny mercy to others is to deny it to yourself.

If you can realize that everything your mother did, although her personal responsibility, was ultimately caused by her own childhood wounds, then you can see yourself in her, and in your sorrow you can have mercy for her. In forgiving her you ultimately have mercy on yourself, and you free yourself of your greatest burden: hatred. And with that weight lifted, you have the satisfaction of discovering in yourself what you always wanted from your mother anyway: real love.

So remember, to despise yourself is to hide your anger at the world and to run from mercy and forgiveness. If, however, you stop running in fear and learn to live an emotionally honest life, you can then, in mercy, call others into honesty and out of their own illusory social identifications as well. And that's important, because when you reject forgiveness for others, you reject if for yourself, but when you call others to accept accountability for their lives, you discover real love for yourself as well.

19 PEACE

To love is to be giving, and to be giving is to act with patience, kindness, mercy, compassion, understanding, and, ultimately, forgiveness. Activists, by definition, don't love—they demand.

And so we have to accept the fact that peace cannot be attained through lawsuits, protest, or terrorism. The only path to peace is through the purification of your own heart.

PEACE is given only to those of good will; that is, those who *will* to do God's will. Peace isn't something that God can just hand us on a silver platter simply because we are all his "people." After all, if God made us do something against our will it wouldn't be a genuine act of love.

Therefore peace—mental, spiritual, or social—really depends on freely willing to do God's will.

- We cannot have peace by trying to build it as an end in itself.

- We cannot have peace by trying to follow a

conscience uninformed by God's will.

- We shall have peace only through obedience to God by using our free will to empty ourselves of all that is not God's will.

IRONICALLY, the very fact that so many people look for easier—and contradictory—ways to "make" peace through human effort is the reason there isn't peace in the world in the first place.

EVEN atheists perform political works of social justice, but their hidden unconscious motive is to compensate psychologically for their spiritual emptiness that is a private, interior terror for them. In other words, the motive for social peace can easily derive from a narcissistic attempt to make yourself feel useful and wanted. That's a hard statement, but only when you have learned to "deny yourself" according to genuine religion will you understand the difference between *love* and *pride*—and the difference between *justice* and *terrorism*.

PEACE is not the comfort of having everything go smoothly, just as you would like it to go; peace is the confidence—the peace of heart and mind—of believing that no matter what happens, no matter how much a trial it may be, God will give you the courage and strength to do whatever needs to be done to fulfill His will.

IN all of this, there is only one truth: *If you want to change the world, begin by changing yourself.* If you want the world to be more fair, treat the world fairly even when you are treated unfairly. If you want the world to be more kind, treat the world with kindness and return a blessing for every insult. If you want peace on earth, let there be peace in your own heart. Show the world by your good actions— not by empty protest or violence—that you are willing to *live* according to what you profess to *believe.*

YOU have no control over what someone does when you are not present, but when someone does something in your presence that you find contrary to your moral values, then have courage and say, "I cannot accept this behavior," and get up and leave. Don't leave in a huff, and don't leave with indignation; leave with gentleness and kindness. But leave. If you stay and say nothing, in a misguided attempt to "keep the peace," you will give the impression that you condone the behavior, and that hurts both of you.

When children are involved, then be honest. Tell the children that the behavior is wrong, let them know that you cannot change the behavior of another person, admit that you feel frustrated, and tell the children to pray for the offender. If the children have been so hardened already that they don't want to pray for anyone, then, in your being honest, you have at least given the children reason *not* to believe that they are crazy for seeing what almost no one else will admit.

And how do you make peace with yourself for having previously allowed misconduct "without any consequence"? You tell the children openly and honestly that you made a mistake. By admitting the truth to them (and you can believe that they already know the truth anyway), you make peace with yourself because finally you have had the courage to face the truth of your own dishonesty.

20   PRAYER

IF you truly open your heart to God in prayer, you will be immune to feelings of loneliness, of abandonment, of anxiety, of depression, and of all other problems with psychological causes. Yes, you will have to endure the heavy weight of living in the midst of the world's sacrilege—but even that is anguish, not depression. On the other hand, if you neglect prayer you will be afflicted with all the untreated wounds of your own psychological emptiness.

BUT be careful here. Don't pray to be given material things or for specific things to happen; instead, pray for God to inspire you and give you guidance, and pray for the wisdom and courage to recognize and carry out that guidance.

Moreover, don't expect that God will tap you on the shoulder and say, "Hey dude! This is what I want you to do." God's answer to your prayers will come though ordinary daily events. It will be up to you to open your heart to believing that ordinary events—under the influence of constant prayer—can help guide you. In regard to everything that happens (especially for tribulations and distress), say to yourself, "What is this telling me about myself? What do I need to learn, and how do I need to change?"

To give the pain to God is to stop trying to take matters into your own hands—by hiding your pain, by dwelling on resentments, by protest, or by plotting revenge—and instead to pray for those who hurt you and to pray that you will learn to approach God in humility so as to accept the true and perfect healing He offers us. So pray for your enlightenment—and pray for the enlightenment of those who hurt you.

Pray also for those around you. For example, if you're stuck in a long line at the post office because of a rude clerk, pray for the clerk and pray for the persons in line with you who have to suffer also.

Prayer should be a continuing act of purification, not dry intellectual superstition and pride. Trying to pray without first detaching yourself from the world is like trying to drive a car with four flat tires.

Conceptualize this detachment from the world not as an attempt to show others that you are better than the world around you but as a prayerful understanding that God offers you something better than what the world offers you.

Beginners often become discouraged because they

don't *feel* anything when they pray. Some beginners even take this as an indication that they aren't "worthy." And some persons seek out charismatic groups in an effort to create their own ecstatic feelings. But prayer is not a psychological process; we aren't *supposed* to feel anything in prayer. God works His graces silently in the soul—unseen, unfelt, and unheard by the bodily senses. Persevere, though, and the benefits of prayer will become apparent.

IN regard to vocal prayer and mental prayer, it's not a matter of either-or. When the soul struggles through darkness, it needs the beauty of mental prayer (or contemplative prayer) to cheer its heart and help it along. But it also needs the discipline of vocal prayers (or liturgical prayers) to keep it on the true path, lest it decide to chase off after fairy lights in the distance and be lost forever.

MANY souls go to their spiritual destruction because they have no one to pray for them. Imagine that. Pray—not just for ourselves, not just to stretch our desire to see God, not just to inflame our love of God—but pray also for the souls of others who might be lost without our prayers and sufferings on their behalf.

MANY persons who seek to live a holy life, and who therefore want to make prayer a more important part of their lives, wonder how they can tell if their experiences in prayer are truly inspiration from God or whether they are mere psychological delusions.

Well, the best approach here is to look to the "fruits"

of the prayer—that is, the effects that prayer produces in your life—and ask if those fruits are truly meaningful, such as love, joy, peace, patience, kindness, generosity, faithfulness, gentleness, and self-control.

WHEN you are praying and distractions interfere with your concentration, say to yourself, "It's OK. I don't have to repeat the prayer until I get it perfect. My intent is love; I don't have to be perfect to love."

WHEN fantasies and "bad" thoughts intrude into your mind, if you try to fight them they will only get more intense, and you will become more anxious. The key here is to understand that God does not hold against us the things we think spontaneously, nor does He expect us to stop all spontaneous thoughts; all He wants from us is to grow in love by recognizing that certain thoughts are offenses to love and to tell ourselves so.

Therefore, say to yourself, "It's OK. I know these thoughts are an offense to love, and I don't really intend to carry them out in actions. My intent is love; I don't have to be perfect in not having intruding thoughts. So let's return to the prayer."

SOME persons, especially beginners, often complain that God does not answer their prayers. Actually, God always answers our prayers, and yet the answer may not be what we would like or what we are expecting. In this regard, from my clinical work I have seen four characteristic mistakes that beginners make.

- *Not listening.* In every moment God is telling you through inner inspiration how to do His will, but because you don't like what He is saying—or because you're afraid to hear it— you don't listen.

- *Not paying attention.* God often answers prayers through external circumstances, rather than through inner inspiration. When you find yourself in an difficult situation, therefore, it can be an opportunity to gain a grace by acting as a true witness to your faith. But if you're not paying attention, you will just complain about how miserably you are being treated and how you receive no consolation from your prayer.

- *Pride.* Some persons have a deep psychological need to feel "special," and they will pray for things knowing that, if they were given what they want, it would either prove to the world how exceptional they are, or it would give themselves some special reassurance that God likes them. In either case, this is a request that serves the illusions of the "self," not God's will.

- *Testing God.* Some persons will pray for God to do something for them, such as "Make me stop smoking." Such a request, however, is just a way to put God to the test in a no-win situation. On the one hand, if God really were to interfere with their free will and make them suddenly stop smoking, then they would never have to come to terms with the underlying anger toward their parents that makes them continue smoking in the first place. Thus, if God gave them what they wanted, He would be denying them what they really need: spiritual purification from their anger and from their lack of forgiveness. On the other hand, if God does not give them what they want, then they can blame God for "hating" them. This will allow them to believe that there is something "wrong" with themselves, thus allowing them to continue to believe that they themselves were at fault for their parents abusing them—and this self-blame allows them to hide from themselves their anger at their parents: "I'm at fault, not my parents, so I have no right to be angry with them." Moreover, all the while they can hate God for "hating" them. After all, hating God is a way to get punished, right? It goes to show how someone will send himself to hell in order to protect his parents from their own faults and from his own unconscious hatred of them.

MOST persons don't pray enough for one simple reason: they are too preoccupied with seeking the satisfactions of the world. Rather than praying, they spend their time watching TV and movies, watching and playing sports, playing video games, listening to music, chatting on their phones, texting their friends, surfing the Internet, and entangling themselves more and more in their social networks. They waste hours of life daily, and years of life over a lifetime, on things that have nothing to do with a holy lifestyle. It's no wonder that God does not answer their prayers: they turn to the world before they will turn to Him.

FOR some persons—especially those wounded by childhood abuse or neglect—the greatest obstacle to prayer is the irrational (that is, unconscious) belief that they are such despicable and evil persons that God has totally abandoned them and refuses to hear any of their pleas for help. Such a belief derives psychologically from a confusion of God with the "Other" (i.e., the social world around us). In truth, the social world, at its best, is completely indifferent to our welfare, and, at its worst, it "sees" us only as objects to be manipulated for its own satisfaction. In other words, it is not God's rejection of you but sin itself—the rejection of God by the "Other"—that has abused you.

HOW many persons say that they trust in God as a rote part of their prayers? Yet how many of these same persons fly into a panic when some difficulty or trial afflicts them? Immediately, they want to get satisfaction, get back at the person who hurt them, or just get anything in compensation. And in so doing they completely forget what prayer is all about.

IN psychology there is an axiom that anxiety and relaxation cannot both exist in a person at the same time; this fact has become the empirical basis for *systematic desensitization*, a procedure for treating phobias. The spiritual realm has a similar axiom: you cannot hate a person and pray for him at the same time. And so, if you train yourself to pray for the repentance and conversion of anyone who insults or offends you, then it becomes impossible to hate that person—and all of your primitive rage therefore dissolves.

IT'S important to realize here that when you feel an insult, it can actually take several hours to calm down. Even though you acknowledge the feelings and the thoughts and tell God that you want to pray for the person and don't want to fall into sin, you might still be assaulted with temptations of revenge for several hours following the insult. It can become a huge battle, but every temptation has to be met with the same technique: acknowledge the feelings and the thoughts and tell God that you want to pray for the person and don't want to fall into sin. Over and over and over.

NOTE that the ability to pray for those who hurt you depends on your being able to distance yourself from a social world that literally feeds upon hostility and disobedience—anger on anger, hatred on hatred, lawsuit on lawsuit, weapon on weapon, death on death—enslaving you to a subversive lust for anger and revenge.

The more that you are able to desire the holy, rather than desire physical, social pleasures, and the more that you can pray constantly, rather than fill your head with popular entertainment, the more progress you will make in overcoming your unconscious slavery to anger and revenge, and the more progress you will make in overcoming your superstitious attempts to wash away your hidden anger.

YOUR son needs to see that you yourself live a holy lifestyle. Your son needs to see that you yourself pray constantly. He needs to see the evidence that you yourself desire God more than anything else. He needs to hear you thanking God for every good thing that happens. He needs to hear you praising God in all things.

If you were a nun or a monk you could pray silently in isolation, but as a parent you have the responsibility to join with your son in prayer in every daily activity. Praying in your bedroom by yourself doesn't help him one bit. Praying silently under your breath doesn't help him one bit. Nor does your participation in any of the common culturally-accepted spiritual mistakes—aggression in sports and games, argumentativeness, complaining, cursing, political griping and protest, and self-indulgence in general—help him one bit.

Therefore, show your faith constantly. Instead of letting your son be seduced by the deceptive mysteriousness of the social world, show him the true mystery of God's love, and teach him how to desire the holy.

NOW, you ask where we would be without protest. Well, look at where we are now, with it: we are in a world growing increasingly self-indulgent, increasingly cynical, increasingly antagonistic, increasingly cold, increasingly brutal, increasingly evil. In today's world, not a day goes by that someone isn't protesting something. And, in the midst of all this sin, look at all the wasted time that could be spent in prayer. Look at all the hours wasted watching TV, playing video games, surfing the Internet, and chatting and texting on cell phones. If all that time were spent in prayer, it would be a different world.

And why isn't all that time spent in prayer? Because real prayer is too hard and demanding. It requires disciplined self-sacrifice and humility. It's far easier to wave a banner in the face of an opponent than to empty yourself in sacrifice before God. Protest feels good. Protest, like junk food, is satisfying—or, at least it gives the illusion that it is.

IN the old days, martyrs allowed themselves to be cut to pieces and burned without so much as a whimper. Today, many of us faint at the mere thought of a pin prick.

Pray for your opponents and enemies anyway, and let your life be a humble example, for them and for everyone. That's what you're supposed to do. Now, and always.

21 PRIDE

So why should so many of us stumble back into the power of darkness? The answer is simple: *pride*—the most subversive of all the sins.

Because of pride, God is betrayed, truth is persecuted, and darkness creeps back into the house from which it once was cast out.

THE brilliant French psychoanalyst, Jacques Lacan, in *The Four Fundamental Concepts of Psycho-Analysis*, tells the story of a competition between two ancient painters, Zeuxis and Parrhasios. Zeuxis receives acclaim for painting grapes so life-like that even the birds who try to peck at them are fooled. In his pride, Zeuxis then goes to look at the work of Parrhasios. But Zeuxis sees only a veil, and so he asks to see the painting that Parrhasios has hidden behind the veil. Well, Parrhasios' *painting* was the veil. It was so well done that it fooled even the master of deceptive painting himself. Hence Lacan points out that if you want to deceive someone, present him with a "veil," something that incites his pride to want to know what is being hidden from him.

SADLY, our entire social structure has its unconscious basis in the need to "hide" feelings of vulnerability and helplessness with feelings of power and grandiosity. Just look at our political system, our law-enforcement system, and our military system. It's all filled with overblown rhetoric and pride.

Just look at some of our most profound social problems today. Certain elements of certain societies feel oppressed and disavowed. So, to make themselves feel powerful, they lash out with terrorist acts. Those who are terrorized by those acts feel momentarily helpless, and then they respond in turn with grandiose acts of retaliation.

So, if our entire culture has oriented itself around power and retaliation as a response to fear and vulnerability, imagine how difficult it can be for one individual to be healed from the depression and grandiosity that result from this unconscious cultural infection of pride.

THEREFORE, unless your desire to make the world change—as you believe it should change—comes from an awesome reverence for the glory of God, and profound humility, you're standing on the brink of pride. Activism is the first resort of those who don't understand prayer. If religion for you is just a role or a job, or if you have to be disobedient or get yourself arrested just to feel socially useful, then you will be imprisoned in nothing other than your own self-deception.

HAVE you ever heard someone complain, "I don't understand it. I give so much to others, and yet I get no recognition or respect. What's wrong with this world?"

Well, the world is simply doing what it does best. It takes anything it can, from wherever it can, from whomever it can, and it doesn't even bother to say, "Thank you." And it's going to keep on doing it, no matter how much you protest. The problem, then, is with the person who confuses *pride* with *love*.

That is, many persons "give" in order to advertise an identity and to maintain a position of power. This is pride, not love, because love empties itself of worldly desires through service, in order to give selflessly. Pride, however, makes "giving" into a form of bribery, in order to get something bigger for itself in return.

IT takes considerable wisdom, therefore, to know when personal need—and pride—are masquerading as social concern. Look closely at some of the men and women in the social justice movements and wonder to what extent they are trying to further their political careers, sell their books, and prop up their own inner feelings of insecurity—or perhaps, just yell and shake their fists for a sweet taste of revenge. For at its core, activism is often just a psychological defense against unresolved emotional wounds from childhood: frustrated by their helplessness in the face of their parents' hypocrisy, activists try to impose on the world their own prideful ideas of what "should" be done.

VIOLENCE is nothing more than a fear of love. And when you fear love, where do you turn? To pride. The pride of your own self-defense.

MAYBE you will say, "Wait a minute. What can I give? I feel like mush inside. I'm already empty. I feel barren. It feels as if I have no identity. I have nothing to give." Well, there is always something to give up, something that everyone holds on to as a final defense: you can give up the pride of feeling victimized, along with your secret hope to taste revenge for all the hurt and abuse you have ever suffered.

IF a person who has been victimized attempts to find healing through psychotherapy while litigation is still in process, there will always be some part of the person that unconsciously desires to remain disabled in order to "prove" the legal case. For this reason, true psychotherapy will be hindered, if not impossible. Vengeance may feel satisfying, but real psychological healing can happen only if the person gives up the pride of victim anger.

WHEN people haven't freed themselves from their illusions about desire, they unconsciously block themselves from psychological honesty and resort to defensively protecting their own egos. That's what your psychotherapist did. Instead of honestly discussing the whole concept of *unconscious desire*, he closed everything down with a defensive denial. Moreover, the fact that this matter has so upset you that you felt the need to write to me points to the probability that your parents—especially your father—must have treated you during your childhood with the same exasperating defensiveness as this psychotherapist. Instead of raising you with real love, they protected their own pride. And the unconscious effect of that damage is now the reason why you need psychotherapy.

THEREFORE, if you complain about how much you are being tested, you are dead. You're simply defending your pride, feeling sorry for yourself and demanding that the world notice your pain. But healing from victimization involves recognizing your feelings of hurt and then resolving to speak about them charitably and calmly without demanding anything. If others listen to you, fine. Work with them to find a solution to the problem, as you have done by writing to me. And if they fail to hear you, well, pray for their repentance and let the dead bury the dead.

ONCE you can easily recognize how the past essentially continues to live in the present, make a conscious effort to resist the temptation to fall into old defensive patterns, and train yourself to act with new and different behaviors. But make no mistake here: this is hard work.

It's essential that you train yourself to make a conscious decision in the moment to bear your emotional pain gracefully, without anger or victimization, but instead with forgiveness. In every moment of difficulty you will, like a frightened child, think first of protecting your pride, but now, with a deliberate act of will, set aside that pride.

FOR you to love God, therefore, your pride must die. It's

that simple, and there is no way around it. And if you say that pride is not an "issue" for you, that claim is itself an act of pride.

GIVEN the fact that God is always pouring down His graces upon us and never ceases to draw us to Him, what, then, would prevent us from receiving those graces? Well, we ourselves push away those graces through our own psychology. Through pride and spiritual blindness—with arrogance, with presumptuousness, with disobedience—we essentially separate ourselves from God's saving grace.

MORE often than not, pride and spiritual blindness harden our hearts to genuine love, and we end up treating God's precious love with indifference and contempt. Some souls effectively defile love and condone sin even as they think they are serving God's will.

The true reprobate, therefore, is the one who rejects love—not because God has withheld it from him in the first place, but because his own pride has pushed love out of his heart.

Nevertheless, a humble prayer for mercy could cast out the darkness to fill his heart with love and rescue his soul from destruction.

MOREOVER, not only must all pride and honor die in you, but you must rejoice in that death as the only path to holiness.

PRAYER, although not much understood in the field of

psychology, is an extraordinary—and I mean that literally: extra-ordinary, beyond the ordinary—form of cognitive-behavioral treatment. It can free you from all neurotic anxiety if you pray out of pure love, with all your mind and all your heart and all your strength as a renunciation of your social-psychological identity and pride.

THE final irony is that a *fraudulent* mystic—especially because of the unconscious anger and desire for revenge underlying the need to be seen as special, along with the pride of wanting to believe that he is special—could be vulnerable to *real* demonic influence.

22 ROMANCE

COURTLY "love"—that is, *romance*—is not a pagan concept, and, though it was influenced by Christian morality, it has nothing in common with Christian love either. Like the famous quest for the "holy grail," courtly love is a medieval literary creation.

In other words, the chalice of courtly love—and all the romantic sentiments and eroticism that fill it—is an illusion. It's simply impossible to heal your own emotional brokenness through the body of another person as mortal and broken as you are.

SEVERED from responsibility to the family, the erotic desire for "recognition" in another person—supported by the contemporary social pressure for every individual to be in a "relationship"—amounts to nothing but a narcissistic renunciation of love itself.

BECAUSE romance is not based in real love, romance is, in technical psychological terms, a game—and to play this game, you must put yourself in competition with everyone else playing the same game. This explains the essence of *jealousy*: in your fear of losing what you desperately want, you hate any person who might come between you and what you want.

SOME persons skip from one "partner" to another over the surface of existential pain, like a stone skipping over water. As long as they stay above the surface they're perfectly happy; but when an affair ends, and they come crashing down, they're desperate for the next leap, sometimes searching for a new partner even at the funeral for the old one. Yet sooner or later the stone loses vitality, and with a final splunk falls into the depths of tribulation.

BEING "natural," bodily pleasure can come from anyone or anything. And God knows, some people have tried anything. Literally. That's the real underlying philosophy to the Marquis de Sade's writings, for example. It all comes down to saying, "Anything goes if it serves your pleasure. Any body—man, woman, child, or animal—is as good as any other body."

So there's the natural for you.

And, like all natural disasters, a sexual addiction leaves nothing in its path but a barren swath of emotional destruction.

JUST as philosophers through the ages have noted that we can find hints and traces of divinity in the natural world, so too we all experience a "hunger" for spiritual connectedness with each other and with God, as a sort of deep aching for what is missing in ordinary life. But given our

state of separation from God, and the spiritual blindness
that results from that separation, most of us fill our hunger with what is most immediately available: the five physical senses of the flesh.

THE allure of erotic pleasure resides in immediate, tangible gratification. For men, it can be the thrill of just reaching out and taking what you want, whether it be the body of another person or your own body. For women, it can be physical pleasure, or it can be the satisfaction of feeling wanted and protected. But, however it's experienced, male or female, this "common love" is just an immediate way of getting something that you want.

THE desire for *acceptance* in our adult sexual fantasies reveals a deep yearning to gain access to the unknown and to transcend a profound existential lack, a hunger for the ecstasy of a closeness to others that is sadly missing in our limited, bodily reality. Thus the fantasies intoxicate us with a euphoric and expansive imaginary fulfillment of the physical senses—as with the "hunger of the eyes" in lust. Sometimes the fantasies become so euphoric that they can even seem to be "spiritual." Nevertheless, by distracting us from our true limitations, the fantasies really cause us to miss the whole point about spiritual responsibility. The governing drive of all these fantasies can be represented as an arrow that, in its deepest unconscious sense, does not seek out another but returns narcissistically to itself, in a desire to make itself seen in the presence of another, and thereby to make itself into an object for its own satisfaction.

CHILD sexual abuse, too, is a form of "common love." But whereas most "common love" takes the form of willing manipulation, child abuse is coercive: the abuser preys upon a child's moral and intellectual helplessness. The abuser gets all the self-satisfaction he or she wants and in the process leaves the child with a life-long emotional scar of having been exposed to the manipulative aspects of eroticism well before having developed healthy defense mechanisms to cope with such psychological assaults. The abuser walks away smacking his lips, and the child is left as bones for the garbage.

THE desire for *revenge* in our adult sexual fantasies is very subtle, and most persons either do not recognize it in themselves or they deny its reality. Nevertheless, whenever we experience pleasure by imagining or seeing others *seemingly* having erotic pleasure, we are using them for our own satisfaction, in the expectation of our immediate, tangible gratification, often in defiance of moral responsibility.

PORNOGRAPHY, in its own way, derives from the urge to defile an other. On the surface, it may seem that pornography is simply about erotic pleasure. But when the human body is made into a biological toy, it is stripped of all human dignity, and this defilement is an act of aggression. The hostility may be unconscious or it may be openly violent, but, either way, it has its basis in resentment.

And to whom is the resentment directed? Well, as in all things psychological, the resentment primarily goes back to the parents. Deep down, under all the apparent excitement, and despite the attraction to what is *seen*, lurks the dark urge to hurt and insult—to "get back at"—what is *behind the scenes*: a mother who devoured, rejected, or abandoned, rather than nurtured, or a father who failed to teach, guide, and protect.

The resentment can also be directed to individuals responsible for a molestation that happened in childhood.

Thus, when you feel resentment for some current deprivation—of recognition, guidance, acceptance, resources, or time—old resentments get tangled up with current frustrations and you are drawn to pornography—and even though it may feel exciting, you are really defiling someone.

LIKE men watching birds fly, you saw in those photographs something that aroused your awe. Like men building wings of sticks and feathers, you began to create your own framework for feeling acceptance and "love." And, like men ignorant of aerodynamics, you, being ignorant of God and soul, tried to find love through your body.

In all of your lack of understanding, though, you did know one truth about love: love is a matter of giving. Children know this intuitively when they offer their feces and urine as gifts—the only things they have—to their mother in exchange for her love. This becomes especially apparent during the stage of toilet training.

Ultimately, children grow past this primitive stage of a

preoccupation with bodily gifts and learn that real love involves giving something we don't possess; that is, real love involves giving intangible things (such as patience, forbearance, compassion, mercy, and forgiveness) that derive from divine love. In real love we give what we don't really have; we give away what God gives us. Moreover, through an awareness of real love, we learn to respect our bodies as chaste temples of the Holy Spirit and therefore cease being preoccupied with mere bodily products.

But pornography took you along a different path. Instead of learning to respect your body as a chaste temple of the Holy Spirit, you made your body into a sex toy. You became preoccupied with feces, urine, and semen as the only "gifts" you could imagine. You sought out especially the love of the "mother" you didn't have, and which, despite your desiring it, terrified you.

And there you are today, lacking any meaningful sense of direction, stuck in a body ignorant of its own soul.

IN the clinical setting, many persons addicted to erotic pleasure will confess that, in their childhood and adolescence, they lacked a clear sense of what they wanted to do with their lives. As a way to cope with the frustration of being overwhelmed by the obligations of a life to which they don't feel any commitment in the first place, they turn to a preoccupation with sexual stimulation divested of any reproductive responsibility or commitment. Thus they get caught up in the meaningless euphoria of an impossible quest for a lost meaning.

Thus pornography takes on the excitement of the

search for a stimulating image. Dating takes on the excitement of the search for a stimulating body. Masturbation takes on the excitement of the search for stimulation itself.

CONTRARY to popular culture, even the desire to erotically arouse another person in the context of romance is not an act of giving. The deep psychological truth is that such a desire masks a more hidden desire: to gain some control over our own helplessness. That is, because we as children felt the helplessness and resentment of having our bodies controlled by our parents, as adults we unconsciously compensate for this helplessness by seeking out ways to control others. We can do this with wealth, we can do this with politics, we can do this with education, we can do this with social status, we can do this with physical strength, and we can do this with eroticism. Sad to say, therefore, the thrill of arousing lust in another person is really an act of self-serving power over that person.

JUST as infantile envelopment in a mother can also be stifling, adult seduction has its own dark side: *smothering*. Sexual seduction, at its psychological core, really is a matter of manipulation by the desire of another. And when seen in its raw reality, manipulation is far from being blissful. In fact, it's downright terrifying.

THUS, in all erotic fantasies you take from the "other" some sort of satisfaction that unconsciously compensates for the love you did not receive from your parents. That missing love—that *lack*—is a wound that drives you to fill its emptiness. None of this drive has anything to do with real love, except for the fact that, in all the arousal, real love is missing.

ADULT eroticism is largely based on infantile needs to be received, accepted, and satisfied. When a person feels intensely received, accepted, and satisfied, then he or she is "in love." But sooner or later that intensity will be broken. The break doesn't even have to be the result of malicious neglect; it can simply be the result of a need to attend to other obligations in the world, and, in the person feeling neglected, intense jealousy can flare up. So, regardless of how it happens, as those primitive needs are not met, then the "love" flip-flops into hatred and aggression. If you don't believe it, take a look at the ugly process of our divorce courts for a perfect example. The world is cluttered with broken relationships that began in sweet love and ended in bitter anger and hate.

All of this proves that real love, which is based in giving, not receiving, is pure and eternal and can never flip-flop into hate.

AS long as you pursue sexuality out of a need to be loved—as a form of something you want—you will be led right behind illusions straight into perversion. As long as you try to fill your inner, psychological and spiritual emptiness with another person—that is, through common "love"—you will remain unconsciously broken and empty. Therefore, only a renunciation of what you think you want and a dedication to loving—giving real love rather than desperately searching to be loved—can lead to anything psychologically and spiritually productive, and it's the only attitude that can begin to carry you through the agony of human limitation and mortality.

23 SELF-SABOTAGE

MANY persons have such deep anger at their parents that they unconsciously desire to keep themselves dysfunctional as a way to get back at their parents. Thus they can have the satisfaction of hurting their parents by saying, under their breath, "Look what a mess I am! It's all your fault!"

THEREFORE, the children's unconscious motivation is to show the world, through their own wretched behavior, that their parents are lacking in compassion and real love.

THIS sort of behavior can lead to what is called a *self-fulfilling prophecy*. For example, an insecure person who is intensely afraid of abandonment can so often impute feelings of infidelity into others that they eventually get sick of such suspicion and criticism and end up actually abandoning him or her.

This whole process gets started when you are mistreated as a child in your family. Not being able to make sense of this irrational abuse, you tell yourself, "It's all my fault." Then, firmly and repetitively believing that everything is your fault, you begin to expect abuse—and, sure enough, that expectation draws hurt to you like iron to a magnet.

YES, when you were a child, your father abandoned you emotionally, if not also physically. Maybe your mother abandoned you as well. You found your revenge on them by becoming emotionally closed off; you hid your true feelings from them, and you acted out in disobedience to hurt them.

But now, as you are older, the rage continues. Whenever others offend you, you become enraged and you push them away, just as you pushed your parents away. Everyone who offends you, you push away.

The dynamic of pushing away actually begins as a benign defense in childhood when, confronted with your parents's anger and criticism, you say, if only silently to yourself in frustration, "Stop!" All you want is for the abuse to stop. But then this initial protective act grows into an aggressive act. You slowly transition from passively trying to stop the abuse to actively getting revenge by pushing away anyone who offends you.

Sooner or later, then, you will look around and feel completely alone. "Look!" you say to yourself. "I'm all alone! Even God has abandoned me!" But God hasn't abandoned you. You did it all to yourself. You pushed them all away yourself. You pushed them away in rage.

MANY of your darkest and most hateful thoughts— the thoughts that you keep shielded in secrecy and would never reveal to anyone, not even a psychologist—are triggered when emotional wounds from your childhood are rekindled by emotionally difficult events in the present. Your experiencing these thoughts and fantasies can provoke feelings of guilt, and then, to punish yourself for this guilt, you can engage in self-destructive temptations or behaviors (such as smoking or drinking or gambling or sexual activity or overeating or whatever). Now, you might acknowledge the behaviors themselves, but unless you get to the psychological root of the behaviors, you will just keep repeating them. And what is the psychological root of the self-destructive temptations and behaviors? It is the hate that you as a child felt in childhood for your parents, the hate that has remained an unspoken secret in your heart that you would not dare to reveal to anyone.

YOU feel hurt and irritated at your parents, and those feelings lead you to impulses of hatred and anger. But that is not all. Some part of you enjoys your disability because it allows you a means of expressing your hatred and getting revenge on your parents; that is, you throw your disability back in their faces as evidence that they have failed you, and in that very act of "throwing your disability in their faces" you get the satisfaction of hurting them—and that hurting of them is your revenge.

Thus you have stumbled into the odd dynamic of self-condemnation: in hurting yourself, you find a clever way to hurt others.

SOME persons will unconsciously persist in trying to punish themselves for their failures even though they say that they trust in God. Why? Well, all that self-condemnation is just a veiled attempt to hurt someone else—usually a parent—who failed you in some way, somehow leaving you feeling rejected, unloved, unwanted, or incompetent. If you are blind to this unconscious desire to hurt others, you will not be able to purify yourself from its effects, and it will poison your heart and kill off any love that might try to grow there.

NOW, the especially sad thing here is that, because unconscious desires can't be seen directly, most persons will deny that they have them. But, just as an animal's presence can be deduced by the evidence of its tracks, so desires can be deduced by the evidence of the behavior they cause.

For example, maybe you can't see your secret *desire* to destroy yourself, but maybe you can see your self-destructive *behaviors*—that is, that you smoke cigarettes, overeat, drink heavily, are prone to arguing, take risks, procrastinate, have difficulty finishing projects, can't read maps, harbor suspicions about others, avoid cleaning or tolerate clutter, and so on.

WHAT strange satisfaction maintains all this self-destruction? Well, it's the satisfaction of unconsciously hoping to show the world how wrong it is. Like Hamlet holding a mirror up to his mother, the person trapped in victim anger will hold up his own destruction as "evidence" that, he hopes, will condemn the world.

UNLIKE a martyr, who lays down his or her life out of

pure love, this self-destruction has its deep motivation in bitterness and hatred, and an obstinate rejection of forgiveness.

IF your response is, "Yeah, right. God is telling me that He hates me and that I'm just a piece of garbage!" then your sarcasm reveals the depth of your anger at your parents, the magnitude of your resentment of others, and the pervasiveness of your unconscious tendency to turn that anger against yourself in repeated self-sabotage. Truly, it's far easier to say that God hates you, as an excuse for your hating others, than it is to listen to the depths of your pain and sadness and, in the process, open your heart to genuine love.

UNFORTUNATELY, some souls are so caught in feelings of victimization that they will send themselves right to hell in a futile attempt to "show" God how mean and unfairly—so they believe—he has treated them. In psychological language, this is called *masochism*.

IF you look back on your life honestly, then, you will see times when you felt humiliated as a child. You will also see times when you have gotten involved with bad situations. This doesn't mean that you deliberately wanted to suffer; it just indicates that people most often choose what is known over what is unknown. That is, for children who have experienced some form of humiliation or abuse in their families, even though abuse and humiliation are not pleasant they are known and predictable, and in that sense they're comfortable. And that's *masochism* in a nutshell: preferring (desiring) humiliation unconsciously because it's more "comfortable" than facing the unknown with true personal responsibility.

WHAT is the deepest motivation for all this unconsciously self-inflicted pain? It's the veiled hope that you can make others love you. That's right—it's the hope that others, in seeing how much you are willing to suffer abuse, will somehow be made to admire you—and therefore love you.

This hope of being loved brings us, finally, to the difference between *humility* and *masochism*. To live in humility is to live always in total confidence of God's love, protection, and guidance and therefore to have no concern for yourself when others insult you—or praise you. Secure in God's love, you don't have to base your identity on whether or not others like you. In masochism, on the other hand, you invite others to insult you because, as a psychological defense against the pain of deep emotional wounds, you take unconscious pleasure in being demeaned in the secret hope that you will somehow, someday, earn someone's admiration for your willingness to endure painful abuse.

SO, considering that boundaries have a core purpose in civilization, an individual's lack of personal, psychological boundaries isn't really a true lack—at least, it's not a lack in the philosophical sense of something "missing." Instead, this apparent lack is really a *refusal* to defend one's own dignity. And it's a refusal based on hatred. That's right.

Hatred: a hatred of the self that results from living always in fear because of having been abused as a child. Unable to make sense of senseless abuse, a child, using the full effort of imperfect childhood logic, arrives at the only "logical" conclusion: "It must be my fault. I'm just a worthless person. I deserve condemnation." And there you have it: self-hatred engendered by fear that is engendered by abuse.

SIMILARLY, *procrastination* can be understood psychologically as a sort of mental paralysis that arises when you face the fear of the unknown. It all results because of a lack in your father's guidance when you most needed it. Thus, with no accountable person around, your journey into mature life became an aimless wandering without a guide— and so it can be said that your every action was not much more than a whim. Therefore, when new tasks appear in front of you now, you freeze psychologically. Behind it all, at its core, is anger at your father for not motivating you when you most needed guidance.

Thus it can be said that procrastination is not just a matter of not knowing how to do something, but that it's an emotionally poignant matter of despair about what you do know: it's a matter of knowing that you lack confidence in how to do something combined with knowing unconsciously that your father has failed to prepare you to do anything combined with a subtle knowing that, in your despair, you really don't want to do it right now.

IF you have ever flown on a commercial airliner, you have heard the safety talks at the beginning of the flight. One talk concerns the oxygen masks, which will drop down from the overhead compartment in the event of a sudden decompression at altitude. In that talk, you are warned to put on your own mask before trying to assist someone else.

Do you know why? Well, at high altitudes there is very little oxygen in the air, and the brain can survive for only a few seconds without supplemental oxygen. So, in the time it takes to help someone else who is confused and struggling, you could both pass out and die. But if you put on your own mask immediately, you will have the oxygen you need to survive and think clearly, so you can be of real help to others.

The point here is that unless you take care of yourself first, you cannot be of any help to others.

STOPPING self-fulfilling prophecies:

Begin by accepting the fact that, when you were a child, others inflicted their own internal unconscious conflicts on you and that you were not to blame for their hostility.

Then you can stop believing that you "deserved it."

Then you can stop hating. On the one hand, you can stop hating others for being so mean to you; you can do this by having compassion for their suffering in their own unhealed emotional pain, and you can forgive them for their psychological blindness and failures. On the other hand, you can stop hating yourself for being unable to fix things.

Then you can stop letting your own emotional resentments unconsciously contribute to the emotional chaos of the world around you. You can say, "From now on, I will do everything I can to seek to understand others, to seek their good, and to help them heal from their emotional pain."

Then you can stop unconsciously wishing to punish yourself.

24   SIN

A psychological understanding of the concept could describe *sin* as a sort of *infatuation with the vanity of your personal desires and a reliance on knowledge, privilege, and power to ignore, disrespect, obstruct, or defeat anyone or anything that stands in the way of your getting what you want.* Or, to say it more simply, most people are narcissistically preoccupied with their immediate desires and have little, if any, altruistic awareness of anyone or anything else around them. Psychologically, this behavior allows you to feel good about yourself (that is, to feel strong and "in control") by using, hurting, or neglecting someone else. Sin therefore leads you away from real love and compassion, and it sends you right into all the predicaments of self-indulgence. Sin really does hurt others because sin defiles love.

WHEN you are in a state of grace, you are in a state of mind and heart to receive the graces God continuously pours out upon *all* of his creation. If you are not in a state of grace—that is, when you are living in sin—you cut yourself off from accepting God's graces. God doesn't *stop* his graces because of your disobedience; you *reject* those graces through your own disobedience.

WE are all basically good. But goodness takes work—lots of work. Hard work. And self-restraint. For without our restraining the pride of self and its defenses, real love, the most exquisite and pure love imaginable, remains invisible. Along the path of least resistance—the path of sin, the easy way, the way to nowhere—love is nowhere to be seen, for it remains banished behind the thorny hedges of psychological defenses.

And what is real love, if not to give of yourself to save others—even those who hate you—from their spiritual blindness?

IN this modern world, though, much of our society has lost its sense of soul.

Furthermore, with the loss of soul many of us today have also discarded the concept of *sin*—which, in psychological language, is a functional narcissism in all of us which serves the self, rather than others. So, instead of making life's decisions according to personal responsibility, we make decisions according to personal convenience. Sin, therefore, is what blinds us to the realization that there's more to life than the veil of the psychological "self" that the world shows us as the coveted image of *happiness*. As such, sin pulls us away from real love and sucks us down into the hedonistic mire of narcissism—and there, in that foul netherworld, soul is lost.

Sin may be convenient, but it's just not practical.

Now, to live a holy life, we must avoid contamination by anything unholy. Unlike medical infection, however, spiritual "infection" does not come specifically from physical contact with other persons. Nor does it come from physical contact with "unclean" things. Spiritual infection comes from contact with the *desire to sin.*

Please understand here that *desire* is not a bad thing. God created us so that we could desire Him through pure love. But our desire for God is obscured by our desire for sin. And so, to live a holy life we must detach ourselves from the *desire to sin* while simultaneously nurturing an ardent *desire for the holy.*

Detachment from the desire to sin, though, does not mean that you are necessarily obligated literally to avoid those persons caught up in sin—and it certainly does not mean that you should hate or despise others. Instead, you should endeavor to avoid the sinful desires of other persons while, out of love for them, also praying for their enlightenment and repentance.

Therefore, you certainly can "yield to, receive, and reflect God's love for the world through the selfless avenues of truth, gentleness, compassion, grace, sacrifice, and wisdom." You do this by a humble detachment from the desire to sin while praying constantly for those caught up in the desire to sin. That's love. It's not a paradox, but it is often misunderstood by those who don't want to do the hard work of praying constantly with the mind in the heart because, in not detaching themselves from the world, they continue in their desire to sin—and thus they are self-deceived.

So, what has this mixture of science, art, and theology taught me? Well, it has taught me that science is trapped within the box of sin and, despite its most powerful instruments, science cannot see outside the box of a fallen world. That, simply put, is the realistic limitation of science.

We would do well, then, to pay attention to sin today while remembering that crossing the barrier between sin and spirituality is a simple matter of personal choice, with complete freedom to go in either direction. Psychology has too often been preoccupied with the pursuit of happiness, and it has missed the point about helping individuals understand life and find a personally meaningful—and practical—sense of direction. Psychology in itself cannot offer any meaning to life, but it can help individuals disentangle themselves from the snare of illusory social identifications that keep us trapped in spiritual blindness and pull us backwards into self-destruction.

Was Mary Magdalene really a prostitute? Well, just consider any of the stars of the entertainment media today who fill the supermarket tabloids and celebrity magazines with scandal and gossip. Are they prostitutes? Or are they just broken, lost souls, possessed by decadence and sin, hiding their emotional pain behind empty illusions of vanity and glamor?

God's love for us is not an "anything goes, I'm OK,

you're OK" kind of sentimental acceptance. To say that God loves us means that God calls us away from our sins into a life of holiness.

CHILDREN who grow up in dysfunctional families often have a hard time with this. In compensation for all the abuse they suffer in their families, they create the mistaken idea that love has no limits or rules and essentially means total unconditional acceptance of anything they do. But God's love has very clear rules and commandments. Why? Because God is mean and arbitrary, like a bitter, irrational parent? No! God doesn't do anything for vengeance; on the contrary, He does everything to lead us to our ultimate good and purification. In the end, God's love has a purpose to it—to free us from our slavery to sin— and His love calls us to respond to it with unconditional love for, and acceptance of, that purpose.

GOD'S creation is good. God loves His creation. God created us to be good—to be capable of sharing in divine love. Knowing we have fallen into sin and disobedience, He still loves us. But does this mean that "anything goes" and that "everyone will go to heaven"? Well, no. *God loves us by calling us out of our sins*—the very offenses that separate souls from God in this life and in the spiritual realm if they are not repented.

GOD is love, and God welcomes us all into His presence. He loves us as we are, despite our wretchedness— but those persons who do not recognize and repent their sins reject God's love for them, and those persons who reject love have no choice but to flee from His presence.

IF you keep committing the same sins over and over, you presume that you can be reconciled with God without having to change your behavior. You presume that a show of contrition can pass for perfect contrition. But contrition is perfect only when you are moved to such sorrow that you will do anything you can to change your behavior. If you are unwilling to do anything it takes to change your behavior, then you are not really contrite, and you are not confessing all your sins, because one of your sins is the unwillingness to do anything it takes to change your behavior. And what you do not confess prevents your reconciliation with God. Presumption, therefore, is a wicked snare because it can make itself appear as if it isn't even happening.

IT'S a horrifying thought, but those persons who claim to live "good" lives and yet continue to live in sin—even as they claim that it as not sin—are fooling only themselves. And how do they fool themselves? They fool themselves by not taking their doubt seriously enough to say, "I don't know; I could be wrong." After all, once you can say "I don't know" you have only one sane response: set aside speculation and stop taking risks.

THE real issue is about whether or not you choose to preserve your own self-interests by misleading others and telling them that sin is not sin. To gamble with your own life is one thing, but—whether by what you say or what you fail to say—to encourage others to commit sin is too horrible a scandal, and too lacking in compassion, to contemplate.

TIME may heal some wounds, but time alone does not bring absolution for sins. Just because circumstances change and you find yourself no longer committing a particular sin, you are still guilty of all the times you committed that sin in the past—unless you confess the sin properly.

So, think carefully. Freedom from a previous state of sin necessitates a profound change of heart. Unless you can state to God, to yourself, to your family and relatives and friends, and to the world in general that what you did was wrong and that, even if you had the opportunity to do it again, it would be wrong, you have not attained the regret necessary for a real confession.

GOD does not "overlook" our sins—in fact, quite the contrary: He knows that our sins will condemn us to everlasting separation from Him if we do not repent them. But if only we do repent our sins then God will receive us as deeply as if we had never sinned at all.

THE real point of rules is to help us stay in an enlightened place of humble obedience to love. When you say, "I won't do this!" or "I'll die if I have to do that!" or "I want do it my way!" every I-I-I from your mouth is a defiant expression of *self-self-self* which flows from *pride-pride-pride*, and it all plunges you, like a reverse-baptism, into the arrogance of *sin-sin-sin*.

"I just want to have fun," they say. "I'm not a bad person." Oh, how we deceive ourselves! As if it were possible to commit sin "just for fun" and say it really doesn't matter. Can you lie "just for fun" and not be a liar? Can you steal "just for fun" and not be a thief? Can you commit adultery "just for fun" and not be an adulterer? Can you commit murder "just for fun" and not be a murderer?

IN order to love others in the way of real love, we have to see sin for what it is, in all its pervasive, ugly reality. This isn't at all depressing—in fact, it should be a cause for joy, because seeing sin for what it is opens the possibility of mercy. What greater charity is there than this?

But if we can't see sin for what it is, then we aren't loving our neighbor, we're loving his sin—and *that* is depressing.

ON the other hand, if you decide to step into the front lines of the spiritual battle against evil, armed only with love, be prepared to be despised, calumniated, forgotten, ridiculed, wronged, suspected, and set aside, and unnoticed as the price for witnessing the truth in a world growing spiritually cold because of its seduction by sin.

25 SORROW

THE simple fact is that, just as psychological change begins with painful remorse for one's behavior, the soul, in looking at the corruption of the world, can feel deep sorrow for it. But without divine grace the soul can do nothing about its sorrow; nor does it even know what to do. Yet its initial, tearful cry will be heard, and its journey into the holiness of pure love—and the profound gift of tears—will begin.

UNLESS a person asks for help and is willing to listen to it, there's nothing you can do. This is the pain felt by family members watching an alcoholic, for example, on the path to slow suicide. You can only pray that such persons eventually hit bottom—and that the force of the impact won't be fatal, but that it will be sufficient to crack open their hardened, angry hearts to let in the light of truth.

When that hard heart does crack, the first thing it feels is sorrow—sorrow for all the injury and pain it has inflicted on others while stuck in its own blindness. It no longer blames others for its own misery; instead, it sees the ugliness of its own behavior for what it is.

And so it can be said that the only basis for lasting psychological change is *sorrow*.

FORGIVENESS comes from sorrow. Not sorrow for anything you have done, but sorrow for the very fact that everyone, including yourself, has the same ugly capacity to inflict harm on others, wittingly or unwittingly. Notice the words I just said: *including yourself*. This is where everyone gets stuck, even your siblings, because it's easy enough to see that your mother was hurtful, but to admit that you have the same human capacity for hurt is just too distasteful. In fact, anyone who has been victimized has a human urge to receive compensation, and for you to admit that you and the victimizer are no different from each other—at the human level—is quite terrifying, for it jeopardizes some of that claim to compensation.

THE surest approach to learning to pray properly is to instill in your heart a deep sorrow for sin (both yours and that of others) while asking to be freed from the illusions of your own identity. Then confirm this desire by fasting; that is, by making sacrifices of time, food, and other personal pleasures.

TAKING responsibility for your own life means that you assume spiritual liability for the injurious consequences of your actions. This will lead you to feelings of sorrow and to the desire to do anything it takes to alter your behavior. To shirk this responsibility, however, will lead you into the dead-end trap of victimization.

SORROW means that you feel the pain of all the hurt you have inflicted on others, that you acknowledge of all your inadequacy that you have hidden from God, and then, willing to do anything to remedy the mess you're in, you throw yourself into His unfathomable mercy.

Feeling true sorrow, you can open your mind and your heart to move past your mistakes into purification: to learn, to grow, and to be formed by God.

With guilt transformed into sorrow, then, instead of doing good for others to make them like you, you can do good for them for their own sake, because of your humble joy for what they will gain.

So when you say, "No more sin. I'm sick of it," something in your heart changes, even if your behavior doesn't change instantly because of it. You simply start a process of change by which you learn to surrender yourself completely to divine love, so that desire for the holy becomes your primary desire.

ONLY one thing, though, has any chance of reaching past your children's apathy and resistance: your sorrowful tears of contrition. So weep. Weep for the damage you have done to your children. Weep for their souls. Weep for your mistakes. Let your tears speak from your heart.

26 SPIRITUALITY

IF you value spirituality, what do you have to lose? Mediocrity. What do you have to gain? Everything.

IN today's world, especially in the San Francisco Bay area, we often hear of persons who claim to value spirituality. But in this sense, *spirituality* does not mean much more than an awareness of some sort of "enlightenment" that imbues one's life with an esoteric, otherworldly feeling while making no particular demands on anyone.

IN the 1960s the hippie movement seemingly brought a sense of spirituality into the world. But, grounded in its protest of social hypocrisy, it really did no more than incite us to an adoration of pure physiology cut adrift from all moral guidance. It began with the naive promise that the emptiness of life could be filled with psychedelic drugs, mind-numbing music, and free sex, and it led to rampant divorce and abortion on demand. In the end, the hippie movement shows, through its lingering effects in our culture today, that spirituality, when divorced from religion, is mere psychobabble. And it leaves the body in a moral wasteland.

"WAIT a minute," you say, "the motto of this country is *In God We Trust*. America is a spiritual country."

Well, we can wonder about that. How can the pursuit of "happiness"—with its narcissistic hunger for abortion, angry and hateful protest, social rudeness, political hostility and sniping, violent video games, competitive sports, pornography, erotic entertainment, subversive music, exploitation of the underprivileged, abuse of the environment, obesity, drugs, and gambling—be spiritual?

A shepherd loves his sheep, yes, but he does not just say to them, "Anything goes. Do what you want." No. The shepherd—at least, a good shepherd—has to establish boundaries and set rules for the flock's movements. If he doesn't, the sheep will be scattered everywhere and all the sheep will be lost sheep. So it is, too, with the spiritual shepherd.

MANY individuals will present themselves socially as cooperative and accepting so as to hide their dark unconscious feelings of anger and victimization, and under their mat of welcome you can find quite a bit of dirt.

Being "nice," therefore, doesn't really amount to much spiritually.

OCCASIONALLY you might hear about a person who commits a crime or is implicated in a scandal. Friends and family may rush to the defense, saying "It couldn't be true!

He is so religious and so devoted to his family." Well, sad to say, it could very well be that a lewd or criminal *ego state* exists side-by-side with the pillar-of-the-community *ego state*. Therefore, a person's behavior in one situation does not "prove" anything about the rest of his or her life.

This all goes to show that unless your values embrace all your ego states you will always be vulnerable to the "snares" of corruption. It takes considerable discipline to communicate with and heal all the aspects of your personality so as to live a truly honest and spiritual life.

TRUE spirituality must have a psychological component. Unlike the pagan worship offered by the ancient Greeks and Romans merely to appease the vanity of the gods— gods who had no interest at all in the moral behavior of humanity—genuine spirituality calls a person into a deep psychological change.

IN fact, the most common impediment to spiritual progress is this: the grudge that chains you to the past.

LUST. Competition. Vengeance. Three sins, any one of which will stop any man dead in his tracks on the spiritual Way of Perfection.

YOU offer a perfect testimony to the fact that no matter how well-educated we may be, and no matter how much we might think of ourselves as kind and considerate, we can suddenly encounter the shocking reality that our peaceful exteriors hide a seething mass of unconscious anger.

In fact, many persons—not just the laity but also the religious, sad to say—use an exterior of spiritual "niceness" to hide some very ugly emotions.

TRUE spirituality expressed in religion—that is, faithful service to God through devout worship—requires complete denial of the psychological "self" and a profound absorption in divine love. It's not an easy process, and it doesn't work by magic—that is, simply by claiming to believe in something.

WELL, if psychotherapy is nothing more than insight, and if all that you do is dwell in the emotions of what you lacked in childhood, you will get stuck in self-pity. You will repetitiously act out your yearnings for your mother in your relations with others. And all that repetition will take you nowhere but in circles.

Therefore, to break out of that closed circle of always missing the point, it is necessary to act differently. Instead of unproductively and melancholically yearning for what you want, teach yourself to give to others. Now that you understand clearly what you most desire, give to others what you most desire yourself. Become a "mother" to everyone—not as a smothering mother who gives material things only to make herself feel wanted, but as a symbolic mother who gives from her heart spiritual qualities such as patience, understanding, encouragement, kindness, forbearance and forgiveness. Giving from your heart like this for the good of others, regardless of what others do to you, is called love, and through real love you will attain a closeness to others that is more enormous than you can imagine.

So, how can you tell if your spiritual aspirations are genuine or if they are merely defensive? Well, the only way is to look for their fruits. If your spiritual aspirations produce socially beneficial qualities in you such as love, joy, peace, patience, kindness, generosity, faithfulness, gentleness, and self-control, then they can be considered to be something more than a mere psychological defense. In contrast, if you are overcome by qualities such as impatience, distractibility, impulsiveness, demandingness, conflict, discord, and scorn for others, then you are growing weeds, not fruit.

And don't be deceived. You will tell yourself that you have progressed spiritually beyond the desire for revenge. But you aren't as advanced spiritually as you think, and you aren't past revenge, because even self-destruction is a cunning, unconscious way to hurt those who hurt you. By throwing your disability in their faces, you get the satisfaction of saying, "Look at what you made me do to myself!"

In his fantasy book *The Hobbit*, the precursor to the *Lord of the Rings* trilogy, J. R. R. Tolkien tells of a journey through the dark and dangerous Mirkwood Forest. The travelers were warned to *stay on the path and never leave it, no matter what should happen*. Yet, no sooner did they get started than they spied fairy lights flickering in the darkness. Enthralled with the allure of the lights, they left the path in the hope of discovering the fairies themselves. But the more they sought after the fairies, the more the lights receded into the distance. Then, far from the safety of the path and wandering helplessly in the darkness, the travelers were snared by giant spiders.

Well, the story continues . . . but the lesson is clear: If you forsake the true path to chase after fairy lights, you do so at great peril.

THE essence of it all is that if you miss the initial direction (and this can be taken in the spiritual sense as well), all the rest of the work you do goes to waste.

LET'S pause a bit here and consider the meaning of the word *superstition*. It is composed of *super-* (from the Latin *super*, above) and *-stition* (from the Latin *stare*, to stand). Thus the word implies a "standing above" something, and so it conveys a sort of haughty disregard for rational authority. Thus superstition is the direct opposite of *understanding*, a "standing under," which implies humble obedience.

Because our closeness to God depends on our understanding of God's ultimate plan for all of His creation, anything that obstructs our understanding will thwart our relation to God. And nothing can obstruct understanding better than superstition.

For example, superstition can turn the focus from a thing that helps us be receptive to divine grace to the thing itself. Instead of submitting totally to God in pure love, we can be led astray by superstition into thinking that the things we do make us holy. We end up reducing devotion to dry, external, ritualistic forms of, well, magic.

IN its unconscious dimension, pedophilia is really a sort of sexual vampirism in which the adult seeks to cheat his or her own emotional death by preying on the vitality of young innocence.

Through my clinical work I have seen that fantasies related to pedophilia are "fueled" at the core by feelings of unconscious anger. The pedophile, lacking an innocent childhood himself, craves to devour the innocence of his victim child, and, in devouring it, to defile it. To his conscious mind, all the pedophile sees is desire, and he might even interpret this desire as "love," as the name *pedophilia* (from the Greek *paidos*, a child, and *philos*, loving) suggests. But, ironically, in its deep unconscious reality pedophilia is nothing but envious hatred for the good and the innocent.

Therefore, when priests, rabbis, and ministers molest children, it only goes to show how much they are caught in the grip of false spirituality. Instead of seeking divine sustenance through spiritual denial of self, they choose to deny the good in order to glorify their own perverted emptiness.

THUS the fear of self-restraint holds back many people from any spiritual progress. How can you hear the "still small voice" of God if you're always drowning it out with television and movies and music and sports and all other entertainment? It's simply impossible. To make any substantial spiritual progress, you have to detach your-self from a world that does nothing but infect you at every turn with its sin and corruption.

So, if you really want to finish your unfinished business, accept the fact that you are spiritually blind and that no effort on your own will enlighten you. Let that acceptance allow you to seek the truth with all your soul. Discuss the matter with God Himself. Implore Him for mercy and pray that He will open your eyes and your heart to see the truth. Maybe then you will be able to interpret the depths of your unconscious anger.

It's relentless hard work for both parents—a true spiritual battle. But when your faith becomes your life then maybe—even though it may take 10 years or 20 years, or more—your children will take you seriously.

Then, maybe, once your children take you seriously, they will see that their anger can be healed.

Many persons shopping for a spiritual life will inquire, "This wisdom and peace you offer—how much does it cost?"

The reply is simple and straightforward. "Everything you have: All your heart, and all your soul, and all your mind, and all your strength."

They shake their heads. "No, that's too expensive. We want something the ordinary person can afford."

27 SPIRITUAL GROWTH

IN order to live holy lives, all we have to do is keep before ourselves at all times the desire to learn to live holy lives. God does not ask us to be perfect; He just wants us to dedicate ourselves to learning how to live a holy life.

If you make this simple decision to learn from everything, you will not have to be afraid of making mistakes, and you will find that in due time you will want to do anything it takes to live in holiness. Make your best effort, then God will guide you.

Do your best and let God do the rest.

WHEN something is forbidden to you, you desire it all the more unconsciously.

Spiritual growth, therefore, is not a matter of forbidding pleasure; it's a matter of pruning away useless branches that bear no fruit. Without pruning, the fruit is sparse and bitter; with pruning the fruit becomes abundant and sweet.

This is what *mortification* means: to prune the "vine" so that it becomes more productive.

THEREFORE, when we pray that God would protect

us from temptation, we find ourselves essentially imploring God for a spiritual purgation that, left to ourselves, we would never think of wanting.

LEST our spiritual battle seem hopeless, we have the solution: *deny yourself.* Stop seeking personal satisfaction from life and you will be immune to the unholy desires of the world around you. As you take up the healing of your darkest wounds by surrendering your pride and defensive identity, your will can become aligned with God's will. To do this, though, you must take hope in psychological purgation through your own dark night of soul. If you accept your purgation freely and willingly, with chaste purity of heart and with ardent desire for God's love, you have all the hope and all the mercy in the whole universe available to you in the battle against evil.

IN spiritual purgation you learn to surrender yourself to total trust in God so that, no matter what happens to you, you can bring the pain before God and ask for the strength and courage to deal with what needs to be done.

LIKEWISE, the concept of *contempt for the self* does not mean self-loathing or self-condemnation, nor does it lead to self-punishment. It really means to set aside your self-interests so that you have the time and the inclination to pray for others and be a personal example to them, all in the interest of their spiritual good, and yet to develop your own talents as fully as possible, in spiritually healthy self-love, so that your growth might ultimately benefit the growth of others.

THUS you can see that there is no discrepancy between detachment from the world and holy love for the world. To love the world with divine love, endeavor to pray constantly for the good of the world, and, in order to be able to pray constantly, endeavor to remain detached from all that is not conducive to holy prayer. There's nothing ruthless or cold-hearted about any of this.

SO, if you do spend money on games and entertainment (resorts, sports equipment, user fees, transportation costs), then be sure to donate at the very least an equal amount of money to charity. That donation won't make up for any neglect of your own spiritual development, but it will pay some of the cost of your failure to spend the time praying for the poor souls who have no one to pray for them.

UNFORTUNATELY, there are many persons who don't want to do the hard work of self-restraint. So, sad to say, they take up superficial religious sentiments as an unconscious way to hide their own fears of abandonment and loneliness. Terrified of their own psychological darkness, they pervert religion into a desperate attempt to "feel good" about themselves—to validate their pride and their perversions, not to cleanse their hearts and souls of all that is unholy.

They might act like pious members of their communities, but deep inside some part of them holds a dark resentment that the world has not given them the recogni-

tion that they secretly crave. And one way or another—
through disobedience, through terrorism, or through sexual scandal—their façade crumbles. They talked the talk
all right, but they didn't know the first thing about real
love. In fact, they feared love all along and were blind to
their own blindness.

LIFE'S purpose is not measured by how much one can
accumulate in terms of wealth, or status, or education,
and demanding compensation for lost wealth or lost status or lost education will get you nowhere. Nor will clinging to resentment over your injuries get you anywhere—
except for where a one-way ticket to spiritual destruction
will take you. Life's real purpose is measured in terms of
purification of heart, and this purification happens both
because of injuries and in spite of injuries. If you fail to
achieve a pure heart, no amount of blame or finger pointing will justify your failure.

MOREOVER, this hiding and blaming doesn't stop in
the social world. It even interferes with spiritual growth.
After all, how can you love God when every difficulty in
life is seen as God's fault? "It's your fault!" How can there
ever be healing when those words of blame are constantly
on your lips?

REMEMBER, anyone can do anything for the love of
God; the question, therefore, is not whether you *can* do it,
but whether you *want* to do it. When you're angry at God,
you won't want to do anything. And why would you be

angry at God? Well, you're angry at your parents for being hypocrites, and you're angry at God because He didn't stop your parents from being hypocrites.

So, when your parents are hypocrites, you will hold secret grudges against them, and any disobedience you show them will be your revenge on them for their parental failures. Similarly, a lack of spiritual growth is a form of revenge on God. Essentially, your continued psychological dysfunction and your lack of spiritual purification is your secret revenge at them all.

IN so far as you respond to adversity and persecution with victimization, bitterness, animosity, and revenge, evil has more and more openings in which to dig its claws; and in so far as you respond to adversity and persecution with blessings, calmness, and peace, in total trust in God, you will be purified.

IN contrast to depression, in willingly accepting our spiritual purgation and confronting our own darkness—however oppressing it may feel—we experience love, not anger. Nor does spiritual purgation cause us to feel self-hatred, because the sorrow we feel for our sins and inadequacies, rather than being an obstacle to our progress, is the first step on the path to divine love.

THE truth is that your openness to love must be understood as a continuous process of growth, a process subject to temptations, doubts, and the danger of failing to persevere to the end. Consequently, the success of love in your heart cannot be guaranteed; it must be nourished with constant prayer and sacrifice.

SO please, for the sake of your mental health, and for the sake of your soul, keep in mind that all human accomplishments will pass, and that no matter what you do, someone will praise you for it and someone will attack you for it. What really matters, then, is not the task itself but your spiritual purification in the growth of your faith as you struggle with any task. You will experience joys and consolations; you will experience obstacles, trials, and persecutions; endure all of these things anyway with humility and grace. Never let anything cause you to commit mortal sin, no matter how important the accomplishment might seem to human eyes.

THE ancient Greek philosopher Aristotle taught that if you want to acquire a certain quality, then begin by acting like others who have that quality, and eventually you will develop that quality (*Nicomachean Ethics*, II:1).

In the same way, if you want to climb out of your mental and spiritual stagnation and live a holy life, then start by doing the things that constitute a holy life. All that holds you back is your unconscious pride and spiritual blindness: your continued satisfaction of defending your own self-interests at the expense of others. In this pathetic state, you won't even know what faith is.

But you don't have to wait until you *feel* faith before you can follow spiritual counsels. Just do them anyway; sow their seeds within your soul and soon you will be surprised to see some awesome new growth filling in the bare spots left by your pride. As the growth continues and strengthens, pride itself will wither and be overgrown by holiness.

PRAY, therefore, that the healing process will happen within you. But pray for healing *specifically*:

- Ask God that you will be enlightened.

- Ask God for the courage to see the truth of your life, especially its ugly and embarrassing resentments and temptations.

- Ask God for the strength to not flinch from the pain.

- Ask God that everything you do will be directed to your spiritual purification.

KEEP in mind that God is willing to forgive anything, if only we acknowledge our mistakes and make the effort to learn from them. But if, deep in your heart, you are trying to fool God, you can't learn anything. It would do you well, then, to do whatever it takes to speak about the dark and "ugly" secrets pushed off into the corners of your heart. Seek out purification now, while you have the opportunity to change the future and while you have some hope of spiritual progress.

28   SUFFERING

IF you pray, "Lord, increase my faith," don't expect God to magically anoint you with a large dose of faith. Instead, you will have affliction after affliction heaped upon your head, and as you graciously cope with it all through loving perseverance, you will emerge from the struggle to find that your faith has, indeed, increased.

WHEN you endure suffering patiently and willingly for the sake of the benefit of others, that is *love*. When you bring suffering on yourself in order to win the approval of some other person, that is *masochism*.

ONE particular atheistic natural philosophy teaches that all suffering is the result of desire. Suffering has no value in such a philosophy, so it teaches a deadening of all desire as an *escape* from suffering.

A person will be drawn to these practices, therefore, because they seem to offer an esoteric "spirituality" while making no moral demands on anyone beyond the ethics of non-attachment and acceptance.

But genuine spirituality must embrace the redemptive

purpose of sacrifice and suffering when endured in love for others. Without God, there can be no love, only self-indulgence. And without a proper understanding of love in the first place there can be no meaning in suffering as the only means to overcome sin: that which "misses the point" about love.

A child copes with life by trying to get others to change their behavior, so as to make things more manageable for himself. Persons of mature wisdom, however, cope with life by patiently enduring suffering—without hatred and without anger—for the sake of love itself: to be filled with love and to sow seeds of that love in the world around them.

YES, you could complain in bitterness that you're not getting what you want from life, but if you think about it, the purpose of life is not to get what you want by denying God because you don't want to deny yourself. The purpose of life is to serve God with pure love, regardless of what happens to you or how the world treats you, so that your sacrifices can help to lead others to true healing from the bitterness they feel about their emotional pain.

IN the ancient world, if a Roman soldier commanded you to carry his baggage for one mile, that would be an impossible circumstance; that is, in the world of that time, an individual had no choice but to obey a Roman soldier.

Nevertheless, there are circumstances other than impossible circumstances, circumstances in which we do have the power to change things. Consequently—especially in regard to our suffering—it is important to have the wisdom to know the difference between what you can change and what you cannot change.

For example, on the one hand, when another driver does something rude to you on the road, it is best to remain quiet and suffer (and pray for the repentance of the offender) in silence.

On the other hand, if you buy an item that turns out to be defective, you can return it and ask for a refund or exchange. You don't have to be a "doormat" and let others walk all over you; such behavior is masochism, not humility.

Or, again, when someone next to you is speaking loudly, you can tell those persons to be quiet. If they apologize and quiet down, then all is well, and you have exercised your wisdom. If they tell you to go to hell, however, then a circumstance in which you originally had the power to do something has suddenly become an *impossible* circumstance, and it would be best now to suffer in silence and pray for the enlightenment and repentance of the others.

Therefore, in all things, pray for the wisdom to know the difference between what you can change and what you cannot change. When you find yourself in circumstances that you can change, go about the work with kindness and patience. And when you find yourself in circumstances that you cannot change, learn to suffer obediently, with love.

PARENTS who abuse their children are themselves suffering from profound emotional pain, but, rather than seek to face up to and heal that pain, they express their frustration at having been psychologically damaged—most likely when they were children, by their own parents—by lashing out in anger to hurt and damage the world around them. Children are convenient targets of this frustration because they are helpless and pose no threat in return.

It's important for you, therefore, to understand that when your parents abused you, they weren't trying to help you become a better person; they were simply taking out their frustration on a convenient target, inflicting hurt on you for their own personal satisfaction.

This irrational abuse therefore, has nothing to do with your being punished by God.

You might wonder, though, why God allowed the abuse to happen to you. Well, maybe God was waiting for someone in the family—that is, you—to get the courage to say, "I'm sick of this intergenerational abuse! *I* will be the one to put an end to it. I won't pass it on to *my* children."

Then call upon God's grace to give meaning to your suffering and forgive your parents for what they did to you; that is, purge from your heart any desire to see them get "paid back" for what they did to you, and resolve to make love the emotional basis of your life—and, from there on, pass on love, rather than abuse, to those around you.

MANY persons have to struggle with the suspicion that they may have been sexually abused in the past, and many of them will never know for sure if any abuse actually happened. The psychological/spiritual task here is for them to acknowledge the emotional pain they feel now, to recognize the conflicts that the pain causes (e.g., impulses to promiscuity, pornography, masturbation, etc.), and to then work to overcome the urge to take revenge on the world now because of what they have suffered in the past.

WHAT if it is the devil tripping you up, rather than God intervening for your instruction? How do you tell the difference? Well, you don't have to know the difference. Just accept everything gracefully as a glorious act of obedience to God. If the devil trips you up and discovers that his efforts result in glorifying God, he will get tired of you very quickly and leave you alone.

29   SUICIDE

SUICIDAL fantasies, when spoken in a psychotherapeutic setting, can actually be quite helpful in getting to some painful emotions that have been suppressed through the years. Of course, it can be difficult and frightening work to voice these feelings—and this points to the fact that it's not life itself that is unbearable—as some desperate persons claim—but it's the thought of facing up to one's own inner pain that *seems* unbearable.

IT'S a difficult thing to admit that your parents did not love you. Most likely, though, they *didn't love* you because they *couldn't love* because they were *afraid of love* because their parents *didn't love* them.

And what is the proof of this?

Well, the whole purpose of bringing a child into the world is to take responsibility for guiding an innocent soul into mature purity before God. If your childhood was filled with loving trust in God because your parents lived in loving trust in God, then we can say your parents loved you. But if your childhood was filled with self-loathing, disobedience, insecurity, and hostility, then you have the truth right under your nose. All you have to do is see it.

Yes, all you have to do is see it.

Sadly, some persons prefer to destroy themselves by suicide or by slow self-sabotage rather than admit that they hate their parents for not loving them.

IN sum, all of this shame and guilt points to one unconscious fact about parental love being missing from your life: the urge to suicide is based in the false belief that you can hide the truth of your parents' *missing love* by making yourself into a *missing object*.

ANY actual suicide attempt is really a disavowal of love and forgiveness, because in effect you're denying yourself the very things you so desperately need: suicide cuts you off from any healing you might attain because of psychological change; it cuts you off from all the good that you could do, for the rest of your life, as true payment for your past mistakes; and it is, in essence, an act of hatred, by which you throw evidence of your failure into the faces of those who failed you, as proof of their failures.

IF your pain were to be thought of as a child within you, then your obsession with death as a means to escape your pain would be like a mother rejecting her own child. What greater sadness than this can there be?

Maybe your mother rejected you, and maybe that is the cause of your despair and sadness.

But God is giving you a gift—the gift of gracefully accepting your helplessness—as the means to find what has been lost and to share in God's joy.

So remember, to despise yourself is to hide your anger at the world and to run from mercy and forgiveness. If, however, you stop running in fear and learn to live an emotionally honest life, you can then, in mercy, call others out of their illusions into honesty as well. And that's important, because when you reject forgiveness for others, you reject if for yourself, but when you call others to accept accountability for their lives, you discover real love for yourself as well.

30 TRAUMA

REMEMBER—*an event is traumatic because it disrupts your previously secure sense of self.* Consider that wild animals live with a sharp awareness of perpetual danger, yet most people live with a naive—and deceptive—sense of safety and security to the point of denying their basic vulnerability and fragmented sense of self. So when something disastrous happens, the psychological damage from the shattering of one's illusions about life and identity may be more problematic than any physical damage.

THE world is generally quite stable. We go to bed at night and, when we wake up, we fully expect our slippers to be right where we left them the night before. Without this sense of stability we would be living in an *Alice in Wonderland* type of craziness. We couldn't function.

Yet consider just how fragile this sense of daily security really is. Any number of things—from a car crash to an earthquake—could happen suddenly, without warning, and leave us in chaos. How is it possible to live secure and peaceful in the moment while knowing that in the next moment everything and anything worldly that we rely upon—our possessions and our bodies—can be wiped away?

Well, many persons prefer to ignore that "next moment" and instead make gods of their possessions and bodies. They rarely think of their dependence on our true God—until something disastrous happens; and then, if they survive, it won't be long before they return to their old ways.

To live an honest and humble life, however, each soul needs its own inner sense of confidence to guide it through the confusion of the unexpected. Complete trust in God and faith in the ultimate stability of God is a blessed gift of peace—a tiny whispering sound—that endures behind the noise of chaos.

As odd as it might seem, even something as ordinary as having a tooth extracted can provoke considerable anxiety.

"A tooth?" you might ask. "I don't get it."

Well, think about it. We all cut our hair, and our fingernails, and our toenails. Notice, however, that these things grow back. Teeth don't grow back. Of course, baby teeth are lost and replaced with adult teeth, but once an adult tooth is lost, that's it. Extracting a tooth is like the amputation of an arm or a leg—or a breast due to breast cancer—or the abortion of a fetal child.

Technically, the loss of any body part can provoke a *castration anxiety*. We commonly castrate male animals by surgically removing their testicles so as to make the animals less aggressive or to make them reproductively sterile. Sigmund Freud, in his philosophy of psychoanalysis, gave a psychological twist to castration when he assumed that all young boys felt an anxiety about losing the penis, and that all young girls felt an anxiety about having lost it.

The psychoanalyst Jacques Lacan, however, understood that these sexual images were just a screen covering an even deeper anxiety. Castration, for Lacan, meant the horrifying recognition of our human fragmentation, the very fragmentation that the infant has to "cover up" through its identifications with the world as it builds up a coherent personality.

In the loss of a tooth, then, is a confrontation—an encounter—with the reality of bodily fragmentation and, ultimately, with death itself. In essence, the loss says, "You're not as glamorous and powerful as you think. You're just a flesh-covered skeleton that can break at any time. Your image of yourself is all a lie."

The loss of any body part, therefore—even a dream about such a loss, or even an abortion—should never be minimized. For with the bodily loss comes the loss of smug confidence in bodily invulnerability. If you don't understand what you've really lost, trauma will hit, and it will hit hard.

REMEMBER, worry can make nothing happen except disaster itself.

THE debilitating effects of trauma derive from its ability to overwhelm a person emotionally while driving out any rational understanding of what is happening psychologically. By consciously creating a narrative structure for the trauma—in psychotherapy, in personal journaling, in prayer—you help to dispel the illusion that the traumatic event has control over you, and you cease to be a helpless victim.

THROUGH the process of repeatedly talking psycho-therapeutically about your traumatic experiences, several things can happen:

1. You can experience your thoughts and feelings in the safety of psychotherapy, and this helps to reduce the belief that your thoughts and feelings are dangerous.

2. You can become habituated to your thoughts and feelings. That is, much like a wild animal being tamed, you learn to accept your memories without perceiving them as a threat.

3. You can prevent yourself from falling into the habit of avoiding your thoughts and feelings as an unhealthy defense against fear.

4. You can learn to distinguish troubling thoughts and feelings from ordinary thoughts and feelings so that *everything* does not seem threatening.

5. You can learn to transform your feelings of

helplessness into competence.

6. You can learn to think of yourself less negatively.

LEARNING to speak about the non-verbal pain and terror of a trauma provides a sense of *safety*, through an acceptance of your thoughts and feelings as non-threatening; it *desensitizes* you to the troubling aspects of your memories of the traumatic experience; and it integrates positive *growth* into your lifestyle. Thus you can draw wisdom from pain and tragedy.

IF everything is accepted with complete faith, none of it has to become a psychiatric disorder.

ANXIETY and nightmares following a trauma can often be the result of repressed anger, and if the anger is resolved in a spiritual context, rather than suppressed with medication, the psychiatric disorder of Posttraumatic Stress Disorder (PTSD) will resolve right along with the anger. Similarly, depression is often the result of anger turned inwards; it can derive from a desperate need for social approval and a self-condemnation for not receiving that approval. But if you seek only God, not the approval of world, you have no reason for anger and no reason to condemn yourself.

RELIGIOUS mystics have said for ages that you only begin to live when you learn to die to yourself in every moment. So when your life is motivated by pure faith, hope, and love, when you *are* prepared to die in any moment, and when death is no longer a fearful, ugly mystery, trauma has no place to sink its claws in you.

THE truth of the matter is that a life unprepared to die—or unprepared for the death of someone close—is not much of a life in the first place. It's a life whose first impulse is denial. It's a life just waiting to be slapped in the face with trauma. In contrast, some of the saints lived lives of perfect joy and peace because they lived as if they were dying in every moment.

So, to have a family life that is truly intimate, learn to talk about death. Learn to ask *"What would you do if . . . ?"* questions. Learn to walk out the door with the awareness that you might not come back. Because it might be the last thing you ever do.

31 TRUST

WHEN the Roman Empire collapsed as a result of barbarian invasions and the destruction of Rome, all of the technological expertise of the Roman culture was lost as well. In the following centuries, the Dark Ages of Western Europe were dark because of the loss of *secular* learning. But there was no loss of faith.

Today, we are awash in secular technology. We are so overly dependent on trust in gadgets—and the glorification of the self that they buttress—that most persons have lost any sense of trust in God. And so we are on the brink of a new Dark Age—a *spiritual* Dark Age of ingratitude, insolence, and atheism, lost in its own spiritual blindness.

SO it's odd, isn't it, that the society around us can essentially make us feel guilty if we don't want to sin. And it does this precisely by selfishly playing upon our fear that *our* existence depends on *its* happy existence, thereby, like a wolf in shepherd's clothing, leading us away from any trust in God.

THE root of anxiety is a lack of trust in God's *providence*, such that, when facing the unknown, you worry endlessly about how to "figure it out" on your own. The root of depression is a lack of trust in God's *justice*, such that when encountering any hurt or insult you fall into a desire to take matters into your own hands to get revenge, but, feeling helpless to overpower others, you turn your anger onto yourself as unconscious self-blame.

SOME individuals have the mistaken belief that "trust in God" means to sit around doing nothing in the expectation that God will do everything for us. But this false belief is based in an avoidance of our taking full responsibility for living holy lives that bear spiritual fruits. To trust in God's providence, therefore, does not mean that we do nothing; it means that we believe that, in answer to our prayers, God will guide, protect, and encourage us as we take responsibility for developing and using our talents to serve God.

WE have all encountered individuals who commit offenses and seem to "get away with it." Although the irritation that we feel is justified, we can also be drawn into the desire to take matters into our own hands and get revenge. If we remember, however, that every crime—every sin— every offense against love—that a person commits is an offense against God that will be accounted for during his or her judgment at death, then we can understand that no one can evade God's perfect justice. To trust in God's justice, then, is to set aside our anger for the injuries inflicted on us and to let God administer His own justice according to His will.

WITH a fully-developed trust in God, children will be protected from everything that can assault their faith. To develop this trust in God, however, children need the example of parents who themselves trust in God. But if their parents' lives do not reflect trust in God, the children will see the fraud and will end up trusting in nothing but their own power of manipulation.

TO forgive is simply to stop wishing for revenge or to stop wanting to see the other person suffer in some way. But forgiveness is not blind. Because trust has been violated you cannot just forget what happened or else the same thing might happen again. There's a saying that unless we remember history we will be condemned to repeat it. So let's face it—even though you might forgive a person who has betrayed your trust, your trust in that person has been crushed.

Trust can be repaired only by time through a gradual process of rebuilding. You have to get to "know" the person all over again. The sad thing is that through what you learn you may have to accept the fact that the other person can never be trusted again. On the other hand, if the other person is truly sorrowful and wants to fully admit the offense and do penance, the desire to do so will be all that is necessary to nourish a new growth of trust between the two of you.

SO, considering these things, let's return to your opening

question: *If my dreams are psychic premonitions, what will I do with this information?* Given all the numbers and coincidences, what will you do with the information? Is the information specific enough that you can go to the police and prevent a crime from happening? No? Then when you think about it, there isn't much you can do, is there? If God wants you to do something with the information you will be told quite clearly what to do. It's that simple. Therefore, just pray and trust in God and don't let yourself get drawn away from the path by chasing after "fairy lights" in the dark. If anything, the experiences and dreams can show you how magnificent and beyond comprehension God's creation really is.

ADDICTIONS draw their strength from your lack of trust in God. When you lack trust in God, and when despair is therefore the unconscious essence of your life, then nothing in you can stand up to the overwhelming urge for momentary pleasure and say, "Wait! This isn't right."

LIFE, on the other hand, is an embracing of all the uncertainty of your unconscious, an acceptance of your essential vulnerability, and a willingness to risk everything to trust in something far greater than what you "think" you are.

AND so the lesson here is a lesson about *warning*. If you put all of your trust in your own self-confidence, you're headed for eventual disaster. But if you understand the mystic ramifications of God's love, and humbly accept and surrender to them despite the inconvenience it might cause to your "identity," and let them be your guide in every moment of uncertainty, then you do have good reason to rest assured.

YOU should speak the truth which, in this case, is, "I don't know."

So when you tell the truth you place yourself, along with the person asking the question, right in the place of unknowing—and right in God's hands. And there, trusting in God's justice and mercy, is where everyone should be all the time.

SO if you want to change the world, pray and suffer—because you trust in God, totally.

32 THE UNCONSCIOUS

WALKING to my office, I hear a voice behind me on the sidewalk. "Excuse me," he says. I turn and look at him. "Do you have the time?" he asks.

"No," I reply. "Time has me."

My answer reveals that I am a psychologist—and not only that, but a psychologist who understands his job.

The truth is, just as time is not something we can ever possess, even though we try to fool ourselves by "wearing" it on our wrists like jewelry, the unconscious, too, is something we cannot possess or control.

THE first problem with the unconscious is that it is, well, unconscious. That is, by definition the unconscious represents all that is true, but unknown, about ourselves. So how in the world can we talk about something unknown? One solution to the problem is to deny its existence or to not talk about it.

It's similar to the time at the beginning of modern medical science when doctors refused to believe that bacteria caused infections. Not being able to see with their own eyes any evidence of "germs," these men derisively dismissed the whole concept of bacterial infection.

To a perfectly logical and rational mind, therefore, the unconscious is just a lot of nonsense. Persons of this persuasion can often be found telling others to "stop crying—just pull yourself up by your own bootstraps and get on with life."

Nevertheless, just as housebroken dogs will revert to peeing on the floor in moments of emotional distress, persons who have not made the effort to understand the unconscious motivation of their past behavior will always be vulnerable to repeating that behavior.

This all goes to show that those who say, "Let's forget about the past and get on with our future" are deceiving themselves—unconsciously.

WITH so much of our lives influenced by unconscious motivation, it can be nearly impossible to determine just why a person did anything. Whatever conscious reason a person gives for his or her actions, a dozen unconscious reasons could be in the background. So who's to say what is the legal "truth"?

Considering all this, it can be said psychologically that no matter how much we try to tell the truth, we are always lying. Granted, the lies may not be deliberate, but, in all that is said, there is always something left unsaid. And there is always some motive left unspoken.

ONE time when I was called to serve on a jury, the defense attorney, noting that I was a psychologist, asked me about the "black box" of the mind. So I explained my views

of the unconscious and said that because we are all motivated by unconscious desires, no one can "tell the truth"
as our legal system defines it. And then I said that I could
never accept the testimony of a police officer at face value because even police officers will lie in order to protect
themselves. A hush fell over the courtroom.

I continued, staring at the prosecuting attorney, "Even
lawyers will lie to further their careers." Nervous giggles
broke out.

I looked at the judge. "Even judges will lie if it serves
their interests." The court fell silent.

But the defense attorney smiled as he caught on to what
I was saying. Still smiling, he asked me, "And so, even *you*
are lying?"

"Yes," I admitted, "Even *I* am lying."

Of course, the prosecuting attorney threw me off the
case.

A brilliant French psychoanalyst, Jacques Lacan, has explained the technical aspects of the unconscious better
than anyone. Lacan emphasized the relation of language
to unconscious functioning. Language, being metaphoric
and symbolic, is one step—one large step—removed from
"reality," and in the gap between the symbolic and the real
is all the deception, lies, and fraud of human social existence.

Although it might seem, on the surface, that our lives
are structured simply by conscious thought and speech,
we are really more influenced by that gap between the real
and the symbolic—or, in other words, by what is "miss-

ing" from our lives simply because we must filter all our raw experience (the Realm of the Real) through our social dependence on an imperfect, and often dishonest, use of language (the Realm of the Symbolic).

Therefore, the unconscious is a side-effect, so to speak, of our separation from raw reality because our use of language fails to adequately express our reality. Lacan saw clearly that, because separation and lack lead to desire, the unconscious is primarily governed by "the desire of the Other"—that is, by the social world (the "Other") around us that is lost in its incomplete expression of reality. Consequently, desire could be described as the unspoken—and hidden—aspect of our speaking lives.

Consequently, the unconscious holds the deepest—and often, the most "ugly"—truths about ourselves.

LET'S be clear about what the unconscious is not.

- The unconscious is not something alien to ourselves.
- The unconscious is not, in itself, sinful.
- The unconscious is not, in itself, evil—but, because of our unconscious functioning we are vulnerable to being influenced by evil.

YOU are vulnerable to the influence of evil in proportion to the extent that you are influenced by unconscious psychological defenses. That's a powerful statement, so let's explain it.

Your psychological defenses, like the psychological defenses of all of us, were created in your childhood to protect your pride and ego in the face of assaults from the world. Unless these defenses are altered through deep personal scrutiny or psychotherapy, however, they will continue on into your adulthood, like sealed time capsules within your unconscious mind, where they cause you, no matter how old you may be, to act with the selfish desperation of a frightened and angry child.

Now, when you act with the selfish desperation of a frightened and angry child, you are acting with a raw self-interest that is very similar to the demonic refusal to serve God. In this desperate state of mind you are thinking only of yourself; you aren't thinking clearly, and you certainly aren't thinking about God, and so you are vulnerable to falling under the influence of evil.

THE original source of all desire is God. God, in His unfathomable love for us, gave us the ability to desire Him as the source of all our good.

But the world desires sin, not God. And so all of us are always vulnerable to temptation from the self-serving desires manifested by the social world around us, for we are surrounded by the unconscious influence of a world given over to a culture of narcissism by which "feeling good" replaces the discipline of seeking all good in God.

Therefore, to seek the way of spiritual purification, we need to detach ourselves from slavery to the world's desire and turn back to a pure and ardent desire for God alone.

AS a very simple example of how this *desire of the Other* plays out in everyday life, consider how a child might see another child eating ice cream and then declare to her parent, "I want ice cream!" Psychologically, seeing the other child's desire for his ice cream arouses this child's desire for ice cream. *He sure looks like he feels real good about himself! Give me some of that ice cream so I can feel good about myself too!*

As a more subtle example, consider the issue of fashion. We will seek out (i.e., desire) just the right types of clothing that will make us feel accepted by our peers so that we can feel good about ourselves. Notice here that other persons (usually neurotic fashion designers with their own unconscious needs to be noticed) set the standards, and we, to satisfy our need to feel socially accepted, will desire those standards. In fact, this whole concept completely fuels the success of advertising: we see an item held up to us as an object purportedly representing qualities we believe we should possess, and so we end up desiring that object with the idea that, if only we possess it, we will be socially accepted.

IMAGINE how any child feels in being surrounded by a vast and mysterious world. In the midst of obscure rules and traditions, the child will feel helpless and ignorant and will be driven by the unconscious urge to acquire a sense of power and efficacy to compensate for a shameful sense of "not knowing."

Now, through education and experience, most adults have come to terms with what they know and what they don't know about life, and they feel fairly comfortable with it all. Therefore, most adults, when confronted with a *Do Not Enter* sign on a door, for example, will simply accept it at face value and move on. To a child, however, the words *Do Not Enter* reverberate with enticement. "If they don't want me going in there, it must be something special. I wonder what it is?" To a child, then, "forbidden" usually means "something to be desired and explored because someone else surely must be enjoying it."

This leads us to an odd psychological irony: to tell your child that he is doing something "bad" only increases his desire for it.

OUR wills are motivated by desire, and desire is largely unconscious. In fact, it is through the "desire of the Other"—that is, social desire, such as in movies and TV and music and advertising—that we become "infected" with their desire without even being aware of it. Moreover, there are powerful, unconscious parts inside all of us that are so terrified of abandonment and loss that they will refuse holiness itself in order to seize from the world any satisfaction and pleasure they can get, pursuing their desires at all costs, even if the ultimate cost is hell itself.

EVEN many ordinary, non-abusive frustrations of childhood will provoke feelings of hurt and secret fantasies of revenge. But because children are not usually taught to express hostile thoughts and feelings by speaking about them—and because they aren't taught the psychological meaning of anger, and because they aren't taught the real meaning of mercy and forgiveness and reparation—children quickly learn, through fear and guilt, to hide their true feelings from their parents.

The ultimate psychological problem, however, is that these unexpressed thoughts and feelings get pushed into the unconscious where they continue to grow in darkness, like mold on the walls. It may be hidden from conscious sight, and it may be hidden from public view. But it can't be hidden from God.

That is, unconscious anger, no matter how much you try to deny it, will continue to stain all your interpersonal relationships. With this anger festering inside of you, it becomes almost impossible to give real love to anyone, including God. Right now, when difficult things happen to you, you fall kersplash! right into the swamp of childhood anger.

MOST persons come to psychotherapy with some part of their inner lives wrapped in dark secrecy. And, consciously or unconsciously, they do their best to hide this reality from the psychotherapist and to present themselves in the best possible light.

Usually, it doesn't even occur to them that they should be talking about the embarrassing fantasies that lurk in the dark corners of the mind. Nor does it occur to them to speak about their emotional reactions to the psychotherapist and to the psychotherapy process itself.

But eventually some chance event within the psychotherapy—some frustration or obstacle—will cause such a profound encounter with hidden secrets that everything breaks out into the light. Then, if the psychotherapist knows his or her job, it will be a time for the real psychotherapeutic work to begin.

But if the encounter is missed, or if the client runs from it, then everything will just sink back into the mire of unconscious fears and secrets.

SOME persons, however, will avoid the work of psychotherapy because they believe that *admitting the truth* about their parents amounts to *blaming* their parents. Consequently, they will drive their resentments out of sight into the unconscious. But this unconscious resentment locks them into everlasting *unconscious blame* which prevents them from ever taking responsibility for their own lives.

MOREOVER, even when the unconscious is discussed clinically, it is usually done so (at least in the US) in the context of a theory that idealizes a "caring" (almost maternal) relationship between the client and psychotherapist. As such, the human bond between two persons is glorified. This makes psychotherapy into a mothering process of caring for the needs of the client, and it reduces the "therapist" to a paid friend—or nanny. And what does this result in spiritually? It implants in the mind of the client the subtle belief that a "caring" mother-child bond with another person is more important than a fathering relationship that points to the mystical relation with God.

NOW, for most individuals who *think* they know how to love, and who *think* they live holy lives, their resistance to doing the will of God will be expressed unconsciously— that is, outside their conscious awareness. This is what makes the resistance so insidious; on the surface, every-thing seems perfectly devout and "loving," and yet grave impediments to charity lurk silently in the dark corners of their hearts.

These impediments can be uncovered only through careful psychological attention to the fantasies that run constantly through your mind. It's hard work, because most of those fantasies seem so ugly that you would not want to confess them even to a psychotherapist. But if you face up to them, and if you do the work to overcome them, you are laying the foundations of real love.

WE try to control the unconscious by numbing it with ceaseless activity, entertainment, sex, and drugs and by pushing it aside with political power, financial wealth, and social status. Nevertheless, the unconscious will find its way to leak out in anxiety, insomnia, embarrassing slips of the tongue, accidents, or self-sabotage, or to erupt in physical or mental illness.

SOME individuals use humor unconsciously as an unhealthy way to avoid conflict. From the way they speak, you might get the impression that these persons are always good-natured and happy, because they are always laughing. But if you listen closely to that laughter, you can hear either of two things.

1. You might hear a "ha-ha-ha" sort of giggle at the end of every sentence. This giggle has the subliminal psychological effect of avoid-

ing conflict by telling the listener, "I'm really frightened of conflict, so please don't take seriously anything I say, lest you be offended by it and want to challenge me."

2. Or, you might hear a person say something such as, "Oops, I almost spilled the coffee all over you. Te-hee-hee." In this case, the laughter is used to disguise an aggressive impulse. For example, this person could be carrying so much residual childhood resentment in her heart for the way her parents mistreated her that the thought of her now causing someone else to suffer provides an unconscious satisfaction for the injustices she had to suffer as a child. Thus her laughter reveals the truth: that she would very much take delight in spilling coffee all over you.

SO long as you insist on believing that you are in control of your life, your unconscious will be in control of you.

NO matter how much you may be convinced that your behavior is determined by your conscious motives, you are still subject to unconscious motivation. You may respond, "I get what you say, and I agree that it may be true for others. But I just don't feel that this applies to me." Well, that response in itself is a form of unconscious denial.

WELL, in the colloquial language of Alcoholics Anon-

ymous, you must hit bottom. Preferably, you will not hit
with enough force to kill you, but you should hit with sufficient impact to crack open your heart and let in a ray of
divine light to illuminate your darkness.

Technically speaking, this hitting bottom is an encounter with the unconscious. If you hit hard enough, you
might get arrested, or end up in prison, or find yourself in
hospital. Or, if you're fortunate, you might catch on to the
problem before it gets too severe. You might only lose your
job or suffer a marital separation.

The problem is really a problem with *repetition*; that is,
because some unconscious conflict is too fearful for you
to speak about it openly and consciously, it keeps getting
played out in self-destructive behavior.

So once you do catch on, you have only one choice: face
up to the fear. And I'll be honest here—facing the fear is
a hard thing to do. But if you do it with trust in God and
prayer you have a better chance than most people have. After all, why else are hospitals, prisons, and divorce courts
such big businesses?

WHEN you learn to voice your pain openly and honestly in language, you enter into a psychotherapeutic aspect of the *Realm of the Symbolic*, and horror can be giv-
en containment. Learning to speak about pain and terror
provides a sense of safety through a compassionate acceptance and "taming," as it were, of your "wild" unspoken—
and secret—thoughts and feelings.

Thus it truly becomes possible to draw wisdom from
pain and tragedy. For example, as a result of talking about

dreams, or of exploring mental associations of one thing to another, you can catch a glimpse of the hidden desires that are motivating your self-defeating behavior.

THE unconscious can be examined only indirectly, through linguistic associations, dreams, and behavioral clues. Any attempt to approach the unconscious directly will be met with fear and denial.

HAVE you ever had a dream in which you are a passenger in a car while someone else is driving? That's an unconscious way for you to realize that, in terms of your current behavior, you are being pushed—that is, driven—by some hidden emotional issue. The dream may not tell you exactly what the issue is, but it does give you the clue that, just as you can be driven like a passenger in a car, so your life is being driven by some need outside your conscious awareness. Finding out what that "need" might be is the conscious task of interpreting that dream.

YOU will dream profusely, once you begin to have some curiosity for your inner psychological experiences. Seeking insight from your dreams is part of the process of letting go of your defensive need to keep your own life under your own "control."

Once you accept the fact that your life is largely governed by social influences through unconscious processes, then your dreams will start to give you some insight into these processes. And once you "wake up" to what your dreams tell you, then you can turn to God for refuge from your bondage to the illusions of the social world around you.

A *conflict* refers to the psychological fact that one part of your mind wants healing and health and another part of your mind resists healing. This resistance usually derives from two things. First, because you have been so mistreated by others, in the depths of your unconscious you secretly believe that you are worthless and don't deserve anything good. Second, because you are so angry at others for having mistreated you, you experience a certain unconscious satisfaction in maintaining feelings of victimization so that you can "throw your pain back into their faces" in protest. Thus, to be psychologically and spiritually healed you must recognize and resolve your conflicts about healing itself.

IN fact, individuals caught up in their unconscious defenses don't really desire to serve God. Deep in their hearts they use the name of God only as an excuse to serve their own pride.

IT can make many persons feel uncomfortable to hear it said, but many health problems derive from unconscious conflicts. "No!" they object. "This is not how I want to think of myself—so repressed that I brought myself a great deal of pain and aggravation."

Repression, however, is not really something to be embarrassed about; it's simply a fact of life. We have an unconscious because we use language; that is, because we can never speak our experiences completely, something always remains unsaid and unconscious. And then, on top of this, whatever feelings and experiences we are afraid to express openly and honestly are added to the general reservoir of our unconscious.

Ultimately, though, this repressed experience will "leak out" in one way or another: slips of the tongue; procrastination; repetitive self-sabotage; hostile comments to others that just blurt out of our mouths; aggressive actions—and health problems.

But, if we have some curiosity about the unconscious and seek to understand it, rather than treat it with indifference and contempt, we can improve the quality of our lives—mentally, spiritually, and physically.

WE might wonder what the concept of "born with" actually means. Many persons assume it means a biological predisposition, something "hard wired" into brain chemistry and functioning. But it could just as well mean that the infant has been "infected," so to speak, with the unconscious conflicts of the parents, beginning with the entire process of conception and continuing on through uterine development.

Consequently, I find the concept of temperament, and its focus on the descriptive imagery of surface behaviors, to be of little use clinically. To facilitate psychological and spiritual healing, it is far more useful to understand and heal the unconscious defense mechanisms that motivate a person's behavior.

In other words, labeling a person as choleric, or quick-tempered, or impulsive, for example, does nothing to explain why that person is afraid of facing his or her painful inner emotional experience and why that person is always angry at others. Such labeling can also foster the illusion that "That's just the way I am," as if it were an excuse for not changing your behavior. But if you get to the core conflicts and defenses that maintain your lack of emotional awareness and your desire to "push" others into seeing their own faults, you have the opportunity to heal those defenses and to radically change your social behavior and spiritual life.

JUST as a child who does not understand the concept of dirt and disease will resist taking a bath, persons who do not believe they are governed by unconscious defenses will resist spiritual purification. When confronted by personal trials, they will tend to seek a way to "get rid of the problem." And what a wasted opportunity! If only they would look inside themselves with deep scrutiny so as to recognize and then remedy the unconscious conflicts keeping the problem alive, they could see that the trial is God's way of calling them to overcome old weaknesses and develop new virtues.

WELL, you tried *not* to be like your father. Whenever you avoid something so deliberately, it tells you that there is more going on unconsciously than you want to acknowledge.

So, instead of treating your employee with real love, you treated her with one of your psychological defenses. And everything went downhill from there.

NO unconscious problem deserves to be gotten rid of. All problems need to be treated with compassion and respect. In fact, the part of you caught up in today's problem served to keep you alive in the past. Once you come to terms with its unconscious "message"—that is, the unconscious reasoning it has been using to protect you—it can quietly retire, or it can find a new, healthy protective role in your life. But if it is "killed off" its wisdom is lost with it.

UNCONSCIOUS psychological defenses get created in childhood to protect us from emotional hurts inflicted by our environment (parents, siblings, friends, and others). Because a defense's original purpose is protective, it will be necessary, if you want to overcome that defense now as an adult, to *understand how the defense has previously been trying to protect you.* That is, it will be necessary to *respect* the original protective purpose of the defense.

In this regard, think of the defense as a child who feels suspicious, confused, and frightened. If you try to force a frightened child to do what you want, you will get only resistance and opposition; the only way to surpass the opposition is to understand the child's fear while also understanding that the child's behavior seems, to the child, to be protective. Then you can negotiate with the child to establish new behaviors that still protect you, but do so in a healthy, emotionally honest manner.

Furthermore, respecting the original protective purpose of a defense, rather than just "getting rid" of the defense, will aid you in changing your behavior without invalidating all the skills and talents that the defense has used so far in its attempt (however awkward and childlike) to protect you. Thus all those skills and talents that the defense has used so far in its attempt to protect you can be redirected into new and healthy ways of acting.

Here are some steps to take in the process of discovery, along with practical examples of how the process might develop:

- **Identify the problem and your feelings.**

  I want to go to college, but I feel anxious and afraid.

- **State the negative thought(s) underlying your feelings.**

  "Wanting anything is selfish."
  "You don't deserve to have any ambitions."
  "You will never succeed at anything."

- **Identify the "voice" of the negative thought(s). That is, is it the voice of your mother or your father or someone else?**

  It's the voice of both my mother and my father. It's my father because, as an alcoholic, he passively hid from taking responsibility in the family. It's the voice of my mother in her anger at herself and at us children because of my father's selfish passivity.

- **State the original protective purpose of the negative thought(s).**

  They protect me from feeling hurt by my father when he got drunk and broke his promises.

- **State the current "voice" of the original protective purpose.**

  "We have a right to feel afraid. Staying hidden has kept us alive all our life. If you expose yourself now, we will all be destroyed!"

- **Acknowledge the "voice" of the original protective purpose.**

  "I understand how much you fear betrayal. My father's broken promises hurt deeply. But now there are other means of self-protection available that you didn't know about in childhood. I can learn about them and use them."

- **Dispute—that is, make a rebuttal to—the negative thought(s).**

  "Yes, having ambition is partly selfish, and yet it can also be of use to others. It's also true that if I get a college degree it will enhance my self-esteem

and my prestige, and yet it will allow me to do better work than I can do now. So if I go to college, everyone can benefit."

- State how the rebuttal still fulfills the original purpose of the negative thought(s).

Going to college will protect me from getting hurt; that is, it will protect me from the hurt of "burying" my true talents.

- Predict how you will feel—and why you will feel that way—if you carry out your rebuttal.

I will feel sad because it will remind me that my father really wasn't there for me.

- Validate the underlying truth of those feelings.

I felt very sad all throughout my childhood because I was constantly disappointed by my alcoholic father.

- State how those feelings can now be a positive motivation.

My sadness that my father wasn't there for me can be an incentive for me to "be there" for some-

one else.

- **Make positive affirmations about your deci-sion.**

  I will protect myself by going to college. I will learn how to be assertive and to have healthy boundaries. I will make my best effort. I will not sabotage myself. I will "be there" for myself to validate my own emotional experiences, and I will "be there" for others. I will never forget the betrayal inflicted on our family by my father, yet I will work to forgive him rather than get stuck like my mother in thoughts of resentment.

33 VICTIMIZATION

IN the ancient sense of the word, *victim* means an animal offered in sacrifice. These sacrificial animals, however, did not offer themselves—they were taken from the flocks—and so, through the ages, the term *victim* became associated with the idea of someone who (a) loses something against his will or (b) is cheated or duped by another. Consequently, in modern secular society at least, the meaning of a *holy victim* has been lost to us, and our use of the term *victim* carries with it all the unconscious resentment we feel for being cheated, duped, or unfairly treated. In essence, according to today's language, a victim is someone who has been *victimized*.

Thus, when we call someone a victim today we imply that the person suffered unwillingly and unfairly; moreover, according to modern sensibilities, we automatically assume that this injustice deserves some compensation. If the compensation does not come freely, we demand it. We sue. We protest. We even kill.

This very attitude—this bitterness and resentment for having been treated unfairly—is the poison that prevents emotional wounds from healing.

HOW can you come to terms with the "ugly" part of human nature if you can't see it in yourself and if you can't accept your personal responsibility for constantly placing yourself at risk? If you don't recognize the repetition, all the king's horses and all the king's men—and all the anger management classes in the world—won't save you from your own unconscious efforts to destroy yourself as you remain locked in the dark identity of being a victim.

LET'S assume, for example, that your father is an alcoholic, or that your mother is a sort of professional "victim," always complaining of being mistreated and treating everyone else with an acid tongue. Or maybe your parents weren't quite this bad, but maybe they misunderstood you in other, more subtle, ways. In any event, you have been wounded deeply, and you have suffered greatly because of the inconsiderate behavior of others. You have felt unnoticed, unheard, and unloved. You have felt abandoned. You have felt rejected. So what can you do?

Well, in the past, as a result of all the hurt that was ever inflicted on you, just like your parents perhaps, you felt victimized. You complained about how poorly you were treated. And, in those complaints, you wanted unconsciously to show them—and the rest of the world around you—how much you have been hurt. And, in wanting to show them how much you have been hurt, you have wanted compensation—and, in some ways, you have wanted a compensation that is actually a form of revenge.

OK. So that's what you have done according to the ways of the world. You have done what everyone does in law, and politics, and sports: feel victimized and demand satisfaction for your hurt. And if you can't get that satisfaction, you will become depressed and seek out erotic pleasure or drugs or alcohol or food to try to satisfy yourself.

IF we get caught in feelings of victimization, then, we will always be trying to tell others what to do. This can happen openly through argumentativeness, protest, or aggression, and it can happen in subtle, unconscious ways, such as sarcasm, cynicism, and passive aggressiveness. Furthermore, when others don't do what we want them to do, then we feel even more victimized. It all becomes a vicious circle.

KEEP in mind here that the part of you that falls into rage has the emotional maturity of a two year old child. When you feel frightened, it's as if you become two years old again; you become a terrified and angry victim, and all rationality and trust in God flies out the window. You will attack anything and anyone, friend or foe, to protect yourself in the moment.

It will be important, then, that the adult part of you be able to listen to the frightened child part of you, as a wise adult would listen to a child: with patience and kindness. Be gentle while the child cries and screams. Give the child permission to cry. Then be firm in guidance. "You're crying because you feel unloved, right? Well, to be loved it is necessary to show love to others. So let's dry your tears, understand what happened, and find a way for everyone to be treated with respect."

REMEMBER one thing: the world is unfair, and your psychotherapist should be helping you to cope with an unfair world, not to pretend that he or she can make the world less unfair.

WHEN you're caught up in the unconscious desire to feel victimized, it feels as if your life is being stolen from you. You're always clinging to what you're afraid of losing. You can never rest, and you can never get enough in return to feel satisfied. In psychological terms, when you have an *external locus of control* you essentially live in a perpetual feeling of victimization, always blown about by the whims of the world around you. But when you love—and function from an *internal locus of control*—you lay down your life for others. When you love, you have nothing to lose, because you have already given up your pride—willingly.

THOSE who entrust their pain to God free themselves from unconscious resentment and blame; in letting their suffering joyfully flow through them as a true holy victim, they *choose* not to feel victimized. No matter what happens to them, they never lose the mystical peace of healing through divine love.

WHENEVER you pray for divine guidance, answers will come through encounters with mundane, daily events. As these events occur—however difficult or disappointing they may be—ask, "What is God trying to teach me in this?" Then open your mind and heart to what you need to learn about yourself through your encounter with the event. And grow in wisdom.

In contrast, if you complain in bitterness, "Why is this happening to me? Why is God so mean to me?" you will remain stuck in feelings of victimization and you will squander the spiritual gifts God is giving you.

ONLY by accepting the spiritual and psychological death of your worldly identity can you step outside the victim role. Only when you stop desiring to get anything from the world, and only when you start giving to the world what you don't really "have"—pure, divine love—will you stop being a victim. Only by breaking bread and giving it away can you multiply it.

THIS, then, leads to the psychological meaning of *responsibility*. "Take responsibility for your own life" means precisely to stop blaming others for anything that happens to you. It means that no matter what happens to you, you have an obligation to pay the price of its remedy. No matter what your parents—or anyone—ever did to you, you have an obligation to work in the present to achieve your healing. Even self-loathing and self-blame—even to the point of suicide, believe it or not—are all veiled forms of blaming others as a way to avoid facing up to the truth of your unconscious past. In every aspect of it, then, "playing the victim" only rejects love and denies healing.

IN the practical sense, most victims of crime today are not thinking of the welfare of the soul of the offender. And that's the simple result of living in a world governed by secular humanism according to the principles of aggression, hatred, and vengeance. But God calls us out of this world's culture of death to live lives of peace, love, and forgiveness, always praying for mercy for others, no matter what they do to us.

RESPOND to your hurt by "letting the dead bury the dead." In other words, stop trying to make the spiritually dead—your mother, your father, and anyone else who has ever hurt you—"love" you or give you the recognition you so desperately crave. Whenever you are injured, realize that you cannot call down fire from heaven to avenge yourself. You cannot make the world treat you fairly. You cannot make the world love you. You cannot make the world notice you. Instead, turn all your attention, with resolution and determination, to the real destination of your life where all victimization must end, and where suffering for the sake of others is the only path to real love.

NONE of this is easy. It doesn't happen just by thinking about it. It requires mental and physical discipline. It takes hard work. It takes courage. And, if your father was lacking, then you lack courage, don't you? Therefore, the only way to learn to trust in God is to strip away everything we use to hide from Him so that, left with nothing of our own making—with no arrogance, no pride, no hatred, and no bitterness for what others have done to us—we have no choice but to acknowledge our wounds, feel the pain, bring it all to God, and depend on Him alone.

ABOUT THE AUTHOR

Raymond Lloyd Richmond, Ph.D. holds his doctorate in clinical psychology and is licensed as a psychologist (PSY 13274) in the state of California.

Previous to his doctoral degree, he earned an M.A. in religious studies, an M.S.E. in counseling, and an M.S. in clinical psychology. He completed a Post-doctoral Fellowship in Health Psychology.

During the course of his education he received training in Lacanian psychoanalysis, psychodynamic psychotherapy, hypnosis, and cognitive-behavioral therapy.

His clinical experience encompasses crisis intervention; treatment for childhood emotional, physical, and sexual abuse; trauma and PTSD evaluation and treatment; and treatment of psychotic, mood, and anxiety disorders.

Dr. Richmond has written and maintains a public-service website about the practice of clinical psychology; the website has no user fees or advertising.

22606808R00135

Made in the USA
Lexington, KY
05 May 2013